VIRTUAL MACHINE EXAMPLES

VIRTUAL MACHINE EXAMPLES

ANTHONY DAVIS

opCode: virtual machine examples, by Anthony Davis
opcodebook.com

paperback v1.3, v1.1: December 2019, v1.0: November 2019

v1.x paperback ISBN: 978-1-7343145-0-2
v1.x ePub ISBN: 978-1-7343145-1-9

about

We start with a working virtual machine (VM) and explain the use and building of opcodes for it. I'll explain how I went about adding some very useful features to a language, such as decoupling assignment, multi-variable assignment, short-circuiting operators, string interpolation, *for* loops, scoped *if* expressions, and exceptions. We'll review how opcodes make these things work in a stack-based VM.

This is not about CPU's and their instructions. It also does not explain parsing or cover the langur parser. I assume some programming experience. I also assume you know or can easily pick up some Go language coding without having to explain all of it, though I do touch on some of Go's features.

The working language we start with is langur, a scripting language I built with Go (also see acknowledgments). To make the best use of this book, you'll need to download and install langur, or at least view the source code. (There is much source code not shown in this book.) Instructions for installation are included on langurlang.org and in the download.

Langur is free, open source software (see download for license). I don't guarantee langur to be fit for any purpose. Of course, I want it to work well for you, but you use or try it at your own risk. As for this book, publisher and author assume no responsibility for errors or omissions, or for damages resulting from the use of the information contained herein.

Occasional reference may be made to others' trademarks, such as Windows. I don't claim such trademarks, but does anyone really have to be told that?

This version of this book is based on langur 0.5 beta or newer code. The code you download may look different than what you see here. The website langurlang.org explains the features of langur. Also, the site rosettacode.org has some code samples.

These opcodes are not intended to diagnose, treat, prevent, or cure any disease.

formatting conventions used

Besides Go code sample blocks, which use a monospace font and multiple colors, the following formatting is used within this book.

```
langur source code
Go and other source code
REPL text
```
language structure
opcodes section

files

I'll often refer to files in a langur package with a short path. For example, instead of src/langur/object/object.go, I'll simply use object/object.go.

acknowledgments

Thanks to those who were patient enough with me to allow me to write and publish a book.

Thanks to God for everything good.

I first wrote langur following very useful books by Thorsten Ball (*Writing an Interpreter in Go* and *Writing a Compiler in Go*), but the code is sometimes very different from Monkey (the name of his language).

The font Bitwise (www.1001freefonts.com/bitwise.font) is attributed to Digital Graphic Labs.

The font DATA CONTROL (www.1001freefonts.com/data-control.font) is attributed to Vic Fieger (www.vicfieger.com).

contents

1

general overview

There is a relatively common general process to convert source code into executable (or virtually executable) code, which langur follows. I understand there are many variations, which we won't deal with here.

This is the process for langur. Each step is completed before the next one begins (see figure 1).

1. The lexer produces tokens from a UTF-8 source code string.
2. The parser produces an abstract syntax tree (AST) from the tokens.
3. The compiler produces constants and opcodes from the AST.
4. The virtual machine (VM) uses the constants and opcodes to execute the program.

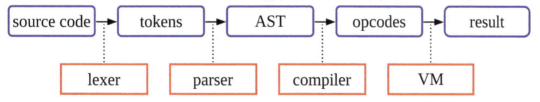

figure 1: general overview

The opcode instructions used by the VM look completely different from the source code. This book mostly deals with the compiler and VM, and not the lexer or parser. There are many resources available on parsing, including the books by Thorsten Ball I mentioned in the acknowledgments.

an introduction to the AST

To compile, we start with the abstract syntax tree (AST) the parser built. The tree starts with a single node. Each node may have more "branches" or "leaves" (more nodes). The whole thing is compiled by traversing the tree using recursion, starting with a list of statements in the program node (the base node).

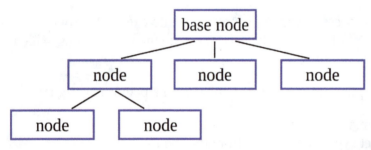

figure 2: AST nodes

Operator precedence plays a role in how the AST is built by the parser. The compiler knows nothing of precedence, but simply takes the tree and compiles it.

If we parsed the expression 3 + 4 x 7, this would build the tree we see in figure 3, multiplication having a higher precedence than addition, and the result of this expression would be 31.

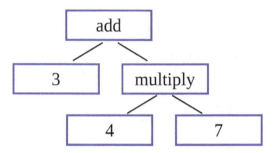

figure 3: tree for expression 3 + 4 x 7

But if we parsed (3 + 4) x 7, the tree would look like figure 4 instead, since the addition is enclosed in parentheses. This would cause addition to take place first, and the result of the expression would be 49.

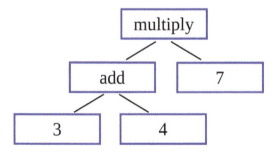

figure 4: tree for expression (3 + 4) x 7

That's about all we're going to say about the AST, except for an occasional reference to it. Let us touch on the compiler briefly before discussing the VM and opcodes.

notes on the compiler

A typical compiler might use an `emit()` function to append instructions to a global instruction set as it compiles. Langur takes a different approach and returns instructions (byte slices) from functions, which can then piece instructions together recursively. This means that we're not relying on a global variable.

Also, because of this, jumps are set relatively, not based on absolute position in an instruction set. It could be possible for the compiler to run through all the instructions and change relative jumps to absolute jumps after everything is compiled, but I haven't done this so far. If it's more efficient for the VM (helps it run faster), this might make sense.

The compiler also relies on symbol tables. We will discuss these things shortly.

2

opcodes

The machine or the opcodes? Opcodes and the machine to run them, may be in some ways analogous to DNA and their biological machines. The one without the other is useless. We tend to focus on the DNA itself, but the code has no meaning without the machine to interpret it (and the machine does not run without meaningful code). The machine and the codes must be designed together to be of any use.

So what are opcodes? An opcode is an instruction for a processor, or in our case, a virtual machine (VM). We're defining "bytecodes" here, since they are not literal machine instructions. We'll generally refer to them as "opcodes" or "codes" throughout.

Each opcode has a given number of operands that always go with it. (It may be zero operands.) The opcodes and operands are encoded together as a slice of bytes (see figure 5).

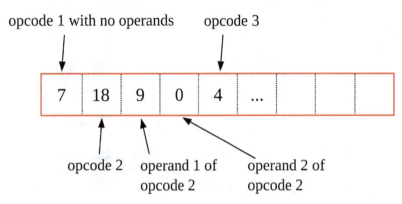

figure 5: bytecodes

Operands are each of a fixed width and may be more than one byte, but the opcode will always be the first byte so that the VM knows what operands to look for in the bytes that follow it. I sometimes refer to an opcode and its operands together as simply an "opcode," so don't let this confuse you. Stringing all these bytes together makes complete instruction sets.

opcodes in langur

A set of instructions for the VM is a slice of bytes which contain opcodes and their operands, all in the order in which they will be read and executed by the VM. In the opcode package (opcode/opcode.go), we find the following.

```
type Instructions []byte

type OpCode = byte

const (
    NoOp OpCode = iota
    OpPop

    OpConstant
    OpClosure
```

```
    OpExecute
    ...

var definitions = map[OpCode]*Definition{
    OpPop: {"Pop", []int{}},

    OpConstant: {"Constant", []int{OperandWidth_Constant}},
    OpClosure:  {"Closure", []int{OperandWidth_Constant, 1}},
    OpExecute:  {"Execute", []int{OperandWidth_Constant}},
    ...
```

You can see all the available opcodes for langur listed in the opcode package.

We use an equals sign to create a type alias (`type OpCode = byte` instead of `type OpCode byte`), so that `OpCode` isn't defined as a type itself. This allows us to freely use a `byte` or `OpCode` type interchangeably.

Each opcode number is from an enumeration as built with `iota` in Go.[1]

Make

An `opcode.Make()` function generates all opcodes. No exceptions. You pass the code and 0 or more operands, as appropriate.

We should generally try to not add too many opcodes to the system. (Try to reuse existing opcodes whenever possible.) With 1 byte to indicate this code, it would be possible to have up to 256 of them. I think we don't want to get close to that number. We could eliminate OpTrue, OpFalse, and OpNull, and generate constants for them instead (using OpConstant to push them onto an objects stack when we need them, which we'll talk about in the "constants" chapter).

---

1   If there was a break between the compiler and VM, and we were to use pre-compiled instructions, we would have to know that these codes would not change, or we'd have chaos. If we expect OpConstant to be the number 2 and it's actually 1 or 3, the VM would mistake codes for something different than their original meanings. This is not a problem for langur to date, as the opcodes produced are only used directly by a VM of the same version.

We could also eliminate OpJumpBack if we were using absolute jumps instead of relative jumps.

All operands for langur opcodes are unsigned integers. They are limited by their byte widths (1 to 4 bytes). Looking at the `Make()` function (used by the compiler only), you'll notice that operands are passed as Go `int` types, which could easily be out of range, which would not be kosher. The `Make()` function checks operand counts and limits (as declared in the `definitions` map). So, if an operand is 1 byte, its value must be within the range of 0 to 255, 2 bytes within the range of 0 to 65535, and so on.

Shortening it a little bit, the `Make()` function looks like this....

```go
func Make(op OpCode, operands ...int) Instructions {
    def, defined := definitions[op]
    if !defined {
        bug("Make", fmt.Sprintf("OpCode %d not defined", op))
    }
    if len(operands) != len(def.OperandWidths) {
        bug("Make", fmt.Sprintf("Operand Count Mismatch ...", ... ))
    }

    instuctionLen := 1
    for _, w := range def.OperandWidths {
        instuctionLen += w
    }

    instruction := make(Instructions, instuctionLen)
    instruction[0] = byte(op)
```

```go
    offset := 1
    for i, o := range operands {
        w := def.OperandWidths[i]
        switch w {
        case 1:
            if o < 0 || o > 255 {
                bug("Make", fmt.Sprintf(
                    "Operand %d on OpCode %s value (%d) out of range",
                    i+1, def.Name, o))
            }
            instruction[offset] = uint8(o)

        case 2:
            if o < 0 || o > 65535 {
                ...
            }
            binary.BigEndian.PutUint16(instruction[offset:], uint16(o))

        case 4:
            if o < 0 || o > 4294967295 {
                ...
            }
            binary.BigEndian.PutUint32(instruction[offset:], uint32(o))

        default:
            bug("Make", fmt.Sprintf(
                "Operand %d of unknown width %d", i+1, w))
        }
        offset += w
    }

    return instruction
}
```

I'd like to tell you, if it were true, that you could change an operand width by just changing its definition in the opcode package. The reality is that you would have to edit the vm package, as well. With Go's lack of conditional compilation or macros, it might be difficult to make it more dynamic without a large drain on efficiency. (But, there is more to Go than I know.)

As I write, the `bug()` function you see here just throws a Go panic, which is like an exception. This helps during development, to catch mistakes. Each package has its own `bug()` function.

3

the VM

The VM runs on opcode instructions as a means to be efficient. Each opcode is just a number that we have assigned a meaning to (a meaning that is the same between compiler and VM).

But, there is more to running a machine than using one set of instructions. We may have multiple instruction sets, constants, a general object stack and variables to keep track of.

In the VM package (vm/vm.go), we have a struct defining the fields for one. We'll be discussing several of these fields momentarily.

```
type VM struct {
    constants   []object.Object
    globalFrame *frame
    late        []string

    frameAlloc []frame
    fap        int

    stack     []object.Object
    lastValue object.Object

    modes *modes.VmModes
}
```

objects

"Objects" (in the object package) are what langur uses for values. You might say they provide a loose type system. The following is just an overview. There is much to explore in the object package.

In the file object/object.go, we have an enumeration for all langur object types.

```
type ObjectType int

const (
    NUMBER_OBJ ObjectType = iota
    RANGE_OBJ
    BOOLEAN_OBJ
    NULL_OBJ
    STRING_OBJ
    REGEX_OBJ

    COMPILED_CODE_OBJ
    BUILTIN_FUNCTION_OBJ

    ARRAY_OBJ
    HASH_OBJ

    ERROR_OBJ
)
```

Any langur object will have a type from this enumeration. You'll notice that langur errors are defined as objects, though the user of a script never sees an error object. We'll see more about error objects as we go, and especially in the "exceptions" chapter.

We also defined an interface[2] for objects, which looks like the following.

---

2   An interface in Go is a type that lists required methods. For example, anything used as an `Object` in the Go source code for langur must implement the methods listed for the `Object` interface, or it will fail to compile.

```go
type Object interface {
    Type() ObjectType
    String() string        // for the REPL
    LangurString() string  // NOT for the REPL
    Copy() Object
}
```

Looking at one of the simpler langur objects, we can see that all these methods are implemented on it.[3]

```go
type Number struct {
    Value *number.Num
}

func (n *Number) Copy() Object {
    return &Number{Value: n.Value.Copy()}
}

func (n *Number) LangurString() string {
    return n.Value.String()
}
func (n *Number) String() string {
    return "Number " + n.Value.String()
}

func (n *Number) Type() ObjectType {
    return NUMBER_OBJ
}
```

An Object LangurString() method is used when converting a value to a string for an end-user, such as when printing to the console, or converting an object to a langur *string* object. An

---

3   There is no explicit declaration that an interface in Go is implemented. It is merely enforced when used in source code. If we set a variable of type Object to a Number, the Go compiler will ensure that the Number type matches the interface.

`Object` `String()` method is used in testing and is intended to give more information (in the REPL, discussed shortly).[4]

One more thing before we move on. We predefine three objects once only and use pointers to them so that any langur objects can be compared for equivalence of *true*, *false*, or *null* by comparing their pointers with a Go equality comparison (`ptr1 == ptr2`).

```
var (
    // reference unchanging Objects rather than creating new ones
    // also, using these allow comparing pointers for equality
    TRUE    = &Boolean{Value: true}
    FALSE   = &Boolean{Value: false}
    NULL    = &Null{}
    NO_DATA = NULL
    // use to return from langur system when there is no value to return
    // no NaN or Infinity types (contained in the Decimal type itself)
)
```

So, nowhere else in the Go source code for langur should we see "`&object.Boolean{Value: true}`", "`&object.Boolean{Value: false}`", or "`&object.Null{}`". Instead we see these referenced with `object.TRUE`, `object.FALSE`, and `object.NULL` (and `object.NO_DATA`).

the stack

To execute instructions in a VM, we need a set way to retrieve and deal with objects. To that end, the object stack, or simply "the stack," contains objects we "push" and "pop" as we execute instructions. I'll refer to this stack often, but here's a brief example of its use.

A stack works as last in/first out (LIFO). That is, the last item added ("pushed") is the first item that will be removed ("popped") when a pop request is made. This works differently than a queue, which is first in/first out (FIFO). The name "stack" is not accidental. It is analogous to a

---

4   The `String()` method for the `Object` interface is not, and must not be, used to generate strings for end-users of langur script files (not used by `object.ToString()`), as that could potentially become a security issue with some object types.

stack of items, let's say of books, on your desk. You add to the top of the stack and you remove from the top of the stack. You don't typically try to pull the book out that is at the bottom. You get to that one by removing the ones on top of it. See figure 6.

the "top" of the stack, where all objects are pushed and popped

The stack size changes dynamically as we push and pop objects.

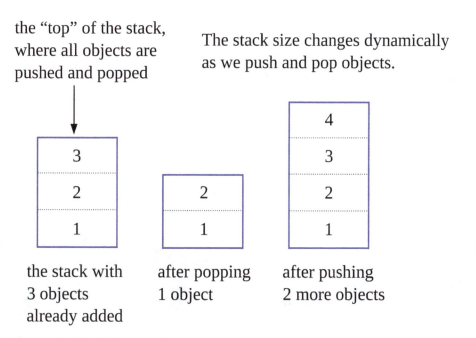

the stack with 3 objects already added

after popping 1 object

after pushing 2 more objects

figure 6: the object stack

Before we operate on any values in the VM, we push them onto the stack with opcodes, increasing the number of elements it contains. Then, a specific opcode tells the VM what to do with those values (compare, add, accumulate into an array, etc.). Each operation will either have a set number of items to operate on, or a number of items given by an operand of an opcode. The VM will then pop the desired number of items off the stack, reducing the number of elements on it.

As an oversimplification, if it helps, you can view the VM as working something like a reverse Polish notation calculator, where each action pushes to or is dependent on values on the stack. There is an example of this in the "operators" chapter.

stack functions

To push and pop values on the stack, we have a few simple methods in vm/stack.go. I'll show the whole file here, as it is not very long. We use pushMultiple() and popMultiple() for simplicity and efficiency when we know we have or want more than one value.

```go
package vm

import (
    "langur/object"
)

func (vm *VM) push(o object.Object) error {
    vm.stack = append(vm.stack, o)
    return nil
}

func (vm *VM) pushMultiple(objs []object.Object) error {
    vm.stack = append(vm.stack, objs...)
    return nil
}

func (vm *VM) pop() object.Object {
    vm.lastValue = vm.stack[len(vm.stack)-1]
    vm.stack = vm.stack[:len(vm.stack)-1]
    return vm.lastValue
}
```

```go
func (vm *VM) popMultiple(count int) []object.Object {
    elements := object.CopyRefSlice(
        vm.stack[len(vm.stack)-count : len(vm.stack)])

    vm.stack = vm.stack[:len(vm.stack)-count]
    return elements
}

// let us see what's at the top of the stack without removing it
func (vm *VM) look() object.Object {
    vm.lastValue = vm.stack[len(vm.stack)-1]
    return vm.lastValue
}
```

What I'm calling "look," some systems will call "peek." I guess you get 3 p's that way.

frames

The VM uses "frames" to execute instruction sets. We start with a global instruction set within a global frame. The VM "allocates" and "disposes" of frames as needed (see "managed allocation of frames").

In vm/frames.go, you'll find the following.

```go
type frame struct {
    base   *frame
    code   *object.CompiledCode
    locals []object.Object
    inUse  bool
}
```

A frame is defined in the VM by a struct containing a pointer to a CompiledCode object, a slice of local variables, and a pointer to the base frame (which is nil for the global frame since it has no base frame). We keep a reference to the base frame so we can access variables defined in other frames. The CompiledCode object contains the instruction set (a slice of bytes) and other pertinent information, such as a count of local variables defined by the compiler.

Scoped frames in langur have their own their own variable allocations (and thus indices specific to their local variables). This includes the global frame (the first frame), which carries global allocations (and global indices refer to this allocation). It might be more typical to include local objects in the general object stack that you push and pop objects on, but we don't do this in langur. To me, it's clearer if we keep these things separated.

A frame's locals slice contains reserved spaces for "local" variables and does not change size once initialized (no push or pop on this as there is on the stack). If a frame does not have variables, the locals slice will be empty. Indices for variables in a frame do not change once compiled, allowing values to be accessed reliably, and changed at run-time when appropriate. We'll see this when we discuss compiling variable declarations and assignments.

code objects and frames

The compiler builds CompiledCode objects, and adds them to a slice of constants that gets passed to the VM. Code objects are for user-defined functions, but also for scoped blocks of code and for a *try* section of code (to trap exceptions for the VM).

In object/object.go, we see the definition for a CompiledCode struct, which includes a set of opcode.Instructions.

```
type CompiledCode struct {
    Name           string
    IsFunction     bool
    Instructions opcode.Instructions

    ParameterCount       int
    LocalBindingsCount int // including parameters

    // "free" variables for closures
    Free []Object
}
```

So, why not just put everything for the VM into a CompiledCode object and use that for execution? The code object contains information that does not change to the VM (all information constant) and could even be used concurrently. A frame, however, has to keep track of local variable values. Many frames may point to the same code object constants, and they can't be allowed to clobber each other's data. We use frames to run code without interference from other running code. This is true even without concurrency. (Think recursion.)

For the VM to execute the code in a CompiledCode object other than the global instruction set, it will call runCompiledCode(). This checks for a parameter/argument count mismatch. If not a function, the argument and parameter counts will both be 0, so there's no mismatch there.

```go
func (vm *VM) runCompiledCode(
    code *object.CompiledCode, baseFr *frame, args, late []object.Object) (
    fnReturn object.Object, relay *jumpRelay, err error) {

    if len(args) != code.ParameterCount {
        name := "f"
        if code.Name != "" {
            name = "." + code.Name
        }
        return nil, nil,
            object.NewError(object.ERR_ARGUMENTS, name,
                fmt.Sprintf(
                    "Arg/Param Mismatch, expected=%d, received=%d",
                    code.ParameterCount, len(args)))
    }

    fr := vm.newFrame(code, baseFr, args)
    fnReturn, relay, err = vm.runFrame(fr, late)
    vm.releaseFrame(fr)
    return
}
```

This will give us a new frame, call the frame with vm.runFrame(), then release the frame, so it's all done in an orderly manner. Except for the global frame, all frames are generated and released in this way. The global frame is executed by a call to vm.`runFrame`() from vm.`Run`(), as follows.

```
func (vm *VM) Run() error {
    // to push late-binding assignments onto the stack ...
    // ... before executing the global frame, ...
    // ... which should already contain opcodes to retrieve them
    late, err := vm.gatherLateBindings()
    if err != nil {
        return err
    }

    _, _, err = vm.runFrame(vm.globalFrame, late)
    return err
}
```

managed allocation of frames

Langur uses a managed allocation of frames to speed it up[5] about 30% by reducing memory allocations. We ask for a new frame to run in the VM without forgetting the current one. Then, we execute the new instruction set until it is completed in some manner (may jump out). When done, we release the frame and return to the instructions we were in the middle of, without losing our place. We may have many levels of frames, and will eventually release all of them to return to the global frame before finishing execution of the program.

The newFrame() method (in vm/frames.go) begins by checking if there are enough frames already allocated, and if not, it will allocate more.

```
func (vm *VM) newFrame(
    code *object.CompiledCode, baseFr *frame,
    args []object.Object) *frame {
```

---

5   Someone may point out that langur is slow. So far, this seems to be true, but it is not likely because of what you see in this book (though optimizations could be made). I chose to use decimal floating point as the basic number type in langur. Since processors usually only have binary floating point units, decimal floating point is calculated strictly "in software" and that is very slow.

```
if vm.fap > len(vm.frameAlloc)-1 {
    // adding to a slice with no more room ...
    vm.frameAlloc = append(vm.frameAlloc, frame{})
}
```

Then, we want a pointer to a frame within the allocation that is not in use already. For expediency, we use a frame allocation pointer (vm.fac), rather than starting at the bottom of the slice and looking for one that isn't in use. We increase the vm.fac counter and set inUse to true.

```
fr := &vm.frameAlloc[vm.fap]
vm.fap++

fr.inUse = true
fr.code = code
fr.base = baseFr
```

Having done that, we set up the frame's local bindings. Since we're reusing frames, we also don't reallocate the locals slice if not necessary. Any local values from a frame's previous use are not present, as they are overwritten when a frame is released. Having set up local bindings, we return the pointer to the frame.

```
if code.LocalBindingsCount == 0 {
    fr.locals = nil
} else {
    if code.LocalBindingsCount != len(fr.locals) {
        fr.locals = make([]object.Object, code.LocalBindingsCount)
        fr.locals = replaceNilInObjectSlice(fr.locals)
    }
    copy(fr.locals, args) // parameters as first locals
}

return fr
}
```

```go
func replaceNilInObjectSlice(oSlc []object.Object) []object.Object {
    // to ensure nil doesn't cause panics
    for i := range oSlc {
        if oSlc[i] == nil {
            oSlc[i] = object.NO_DATA
        }
    }
    return oSlc
}
```

The `releaseFrame()` method, called by `runCompiledCode()` when it's done with a frame, cleans up by clearing values from the locals slice, setting `inUse` to `false`, stepping down the frame allocation pointer until it encounters a frame in use, and more, as you see below.

```go
func (vm *VM) releaseFrame(fr *frame) {
    // clean some of frame at release
    if len(fr.locals) > 0 {
        for i := range fr.locals {
            fr.locals[i] = object.NO_DATA
        }
    }

    fr.base = nil
    fr.inUse = false

    // step down fap as possible
    for vm.fap > 0 && !vm.frameAlloc[vm.fap-1].inUse {
        vm.fap--
    }

    // frees some memory?
    if vm.fap*3 < len(vm.frameAlloc) {
        vm.frameAlloc = vm.frameAlloc[:vm.fap+1]
    }
}
```

Even with these extra activities around requesting and releasing a frame, it is faster than allocating a new frame every time one is needed. I've read that memory allocation is slow, and this seems to confirm it.

the instruction loop

To execute a frame, we have an instruction loop to read each opcode (and its operands) in sequence. Each iteration of the loop will execute one opcode. Here is the start of the runFrame() method (in vm/vm.go) that contains the loop. This is called by runCompiledCode() or by vm.Run().

```go
func (vm *VM) runFrame(fr *frame) (
    fnReturn object.Object, relay *jumpRelay, err error) {
```

Go allows multiple return values. It also allows named return values that can be set from anywhere within a function. Then, using return without specifying return values, any that were not set explicitly will have the default values for those types. The default for all the return values of runFrame() is nil.

We see runFrame() returns a langur object (fnReturn), a pointer to a jump relay, and a Go error. The fnReturn object helps propagate langur return values out of a frame. We will discuss that later.

Below is a shortened version of the instruction loop. I used triple dots to indicate that there is more code. We use fr.code.Instructions often, so we assign it to a variable with a shorter name (ins). The ip variable is the instruction pointer, giving a 0-based index of the byte position in the instruction set.

```go
    ...

    retainLastValue := false
    ins := fr.code.Instructions

    ...
```

```go
for ip := 0; ip < len(ins); ip++ {
    op := opcode.OpCode(ins[ip])

    switch op {
    case opcode.OpPop:
        vm.pop()
        ...

    case opcode.OpReturnValue:
        fnReturn = vm.pop()
        return
        ...

    }

    if err != nil {
        return
    }

    if fnReturn != nil {
        return
    }

    if relay != nil {
        if relay.Level == 0 {
            ip += relay.Jump
            if relay.Value != nil {
                err = vm.push(relay.Value)
            }
            relay = nil
        } else {
            relay.Level--
            return
        }
    }

}
```

```
    retainLastValue = true
    return
}
```

This loop will iterate over an instruction set until it runs out of opcodes or otherwise exits the frame. As it reads opcodes, these tell the VM what to do next. We'll see many more opcodes as we go.

return from langur functions

As you see above, an OpReturnValue simply sets the fnReturn value, which is a named return value of runFrame(), and exits the frame by returning from that Go method. The instructions for a langur function always use an OpReturnValue, even if there is no return statement in the langur source code, so it will always set fnReturn, unless there is an exception.

Note that at the end of the instruction loop (and still within it), if the fnReturn value is not nil, we return from the frame no matter where we are in an instruction set.

```
if fnReturn != nil {
    return
}
```

This is because fnReturn is not handled in this loop, but only propagated. This value is caught and handled by executeFunctionCall(). If a frame returns with this value, but was not called by executeFunctionCall(), the frame receiving it will exit immediately and pass it on. In this way, it will propagate until it backs out to executeFunctionCall(). This is because frames are used for more than functions, and the fnReturn value is only for langur functions. So, we know if we receive one of these, it is time to exit the most immediate langur function. We will see more about this in the chapter on "user-defined functions." Other VM's may handle this differently.

jump relays

The other return value for `runFrame()`, `jumpRelay`, is used to propagate a jump relay. This is a `struct` containing a jump distance (in bytes), a frame level, and a value to pass along (could be `nil` for no value).

```
type jumpRelay struct {
    Jump   int
    Level int
    Value object.Object
}
```

OpJumpRelay or OpJumpRelayIfNotTruthy opcodes produce these and return immediately (OpJumpRelayIfNotTruthy conditionally). Then, another frame, checking at the end of its instruction loop (for each iteration), sees that it received a jump relay. If the level is 0, then it executes the jump in the current frame. If not, it decrements the level count by 1 and exits (returning it to another frame).

```
} else if relay != nil {
    if relay.Level == 0 {
        ip += relay.Jump
        if relay.Value != nil {
            err = vm.push(relay.Value)
        }
        relay = nil
    } else {
        relay.Level--
        return
    }
}
```

The jump relay is used with scoped *if* expressions, so we'll discuss it in the "if / given expressions" chapter.

reset the stack

If we run out of instructions in a loop, we know we're not in a function frame, and did not receive an error or a jump relay. We set `retainLastValue` to `true` and exit. And then what?

First note that our stack is actually a Go slice,[6] which we can change the size of dynamically. The old, typical way is to use a pre-allocated fixed-size stack array and a stack pointer to determine the current position. I like not needing an active stack pointer or a preset stack size.

When exiting `runFrame()`, Go will execute a deferred function that was declared at the beginning of `runFrame()`, which we haven't looked at yet. It looks like the following, with `sp` as a stack pointer variable. The stack pointer is not used directly, as it would be in many systems. It is only used to reset the stack when we exit a frame.

```
    . . .

// to reset the stack on exit
sp := len(vm.stack)

defer func() {
    if retainLastValue && fr != vm.globalFrame {
        // reset stack + add last value
        last := vm.look()
        vm.stack = vm.stack[:sp+1]
        vm.stack[sp] = last

    } else {
        // just reset the stack
        vm.stack = vm.stack[:sp]
    }
}()
```

---

6   Slices in Go are like "vectors," arrays that are resizable. Technically, they are 3 pieces: a pointer to a fixed-size array, a length count, and a capacity count. Go reallocates if necessary when you use the `append()` function. If it must reallocate, it doubles the capacity to keep allocations to a minimum.

```
for ip := 0; ip < len(ins); ip++ {
    ...
```

Exiting a frame, the values used in the frame are no longer relevant and we restore the objects stack to its previous state to continue execution.

If we ran out of instructions in a frame, we know that we did not have a langur function return or exception or a jump relay. If this is not the global frame, we include the last value when resetting the stack. Since we use frames for more than langur functions, we need the last value of the frame to persist.

The vm.look() method looks at the top of the stack without popping the value (which we use for other things we'll see later). Using vm.look() here is possibly more efficient than using vm.pop(), since we reset the stack right after that.

4

running langur

I can't cover every possibility or means of installing things in this book, but I hope the following will be helpful.

To build langur, you will need the Go language (golang.org) installed first. If you're using Linux, this should be available in the repository for your distribution. Preferably, also use an integrated development environment (IDE) to make your programming life sweeter. I have been using LiteIDE (github.com/visualfc/liteide), which has worked well for me with Go. It appears there are downloads of both Go and LiteIDE available for Windows, Mac, or Linux.

Find the Go source code folder, which may vary from system to system, and place the "langur" folder inside the "src" folder. Read the instructions with the langur download, or on the website (langurlang.org), to determine how to compile langur. You will likely need to download a couple of other things which langur depends on. These are linked to from the website.

One thing I want to point out about the installation. You will need to copy one set of files from the standard library Go source code files to a folder in the langur source code folder. The reason for this is that the standard library has so far lacked regexp replace with maximum count functions (has replace all functions only). Don't ask me why. We need this to round out the re2 regex features for langur.

This is not hard to do, especially since we copy out of a system folder, not into it. Better safe than sorry. When you first unzip the langur source code files, you'll only see 2 files in the langur/regexp folder (regexp_replaceN.go and REGEXP_README.md). The rest of the files must be copied from something like /usr/lib/go-1.10/src/regexp. This will vary per system and version of Go installed.

the REPL

Before we can get far into code examples and opcodes, we need to know how to use the REPL (**r**ead, **e**val, **p**rint, **l**oop). The REPL is useful for learning and for testing the language.

Once you have Go installed and an IDE, and all the files needed for langur, load the REPL. The REPL will be langur/repl/main.go (not langur/main.go).

In the source code for the REPL, you'll find the following.

```
const (
    PROMPT = ">> "

    printLexTokens = false

    printParseTokenRepresentation = false
    printParseNodes               = false

    printCompiledInstructions = true
    printCompiledConstants    = true

    printVmResultEscaped   = true
    printVmResultGoEscaped = false
    printVmResultRaw       = false
)
```

Set these constants to `true` or `false` before running the REPL to tell it what kind of feedback you want it to give. It uses minimal execution. That is, if you set all the print VM results constants to false, the VM will not be run. Likewise, if you don't need the VM or the compiler, the compiler will not be run. And, if you don't need the VM, the compiler, or the parser, the parser will not be run.

Generally, for this book, you should set it to print Instructions and Constants, and a VM result for some examples.

Build and run the REPL and if all is well, you should get a prompt something like the following.

```
This is the REPL for langur 0.5.0 (langurlang.org).
Type "exit" to quit.
Type "reset" for a new environment.
Type "list" to list built-in functions.
>>
```

The ">>" is the prompt at which we'll enter commands.

In printing opcodes in the REPL, langur leaves out the "Op", so "OpExecute" shows as `Execute`. Each opcode is followed on the same line by any operands that it has.

A 4-digit number preceding each instruction, such as `0007`, is the 0-based starting position (in bytes) for an instruction in a block of instructions. Instruction widths vary by opcode. So, opcode `0001 Constant 1` may be followed by opcode `0004 SetLocal 0` because an OpConstant requires 3 bytes (1 byte for the code to indicate OpConstant and 2 bytes for the operand that gives the index of the constant).

In using the REPL, I'll often enter a number or something for the first entry that you will not see in this book. This is to get late-binding assignment opcodes out of the way. Late-binding assignments are for things such as _env, a hash of environment variables, which the VM only knows at run-time. You won't see these preliminary codes for the rest of the book.

Here is what a first run of the REPL looks like....

```
>> 123
ByteCode Instructions
0000 Constant 0
0003 SetGlobal 0
0006 Pop
0007 SetGlobal 1
0010 Pop
0011 SetGlobal 2
0014 Pop
0015 SetGlobal 3
0018 Pop
0019 Constant 1
0022 Pop

ByteCode Constants
0: String "0.5.0"
1: Number 123

langur escaped result: 123
```

I'll also be removing the "0: String" constant, which we don't need to see on every example.

script files

You don't have to run script files to use this book. The REPL is sufficient for it. It would be good to get into writing scripts, though. If you do create script files, the recommended file extension is **.langur**. Also, save script files as UTF-8 (or ASCII), as that is the only format that langur understands for source code. Do not use a BOM (byte order mark). You may use Linux or Windows line returns.

building langur

You would have to build langur first, and maybe copy it somewhere (the location dependent upon your system). Of course, if you know what you're doing, you could use the command line to do all of the following instead of the graphical user interface (GUI), but I'll just briefly touch on how to do so using the GUI.

How to build langur depends on the IDE you're using. Using LiteIDE, I load the langur/main.go file (not langur/repl/main.go) and type Ctrl-B for "build."

When you build langur/main.go, it will likely be placed in the langur folder, as langur/langur (or langur/langur.exe on Windows). If using Linux, you could copy this into the /usr/bin folder, which will make it available directly from a command line without having to type a path to the interpreter. You may have to open a window "as administrator" to the path /usr/bin, to be able to copy into it. Be careful when you have a window open "as administrator," because you could ruin the other contents of the folder.

langur from the command line

Once you've built langur and copied it to the right location, there are two ways to run langur scripts from the command line (by invoking the langur command directly or by adding a "shebang" line to the script).

Invoke the langur interpreter indirectly by adding a "shebang" line as the first line of your script (such as `#! /usr/bin/langur`), as you do with Perl scripts. This tells a Linux shell where to find the interpreter for a particular script. It must be the very first line. (If you don't add this and you try to execute a langur script directly in Linux, the shell will think it's supposed to be a shell script and it will surely fail.) You would, of course, have to set a Linux file's permission to executable before you can run it directly from a shell. Use something like the following.

```
chmod 755 nicefile.langur
```

Then, in the same directory, use the following to execute it.

```
./nicefile.langur
```

As I write, the langur interpreter does not have an execute flag to execute a script string from the command line, as Perl has (no "Perl pie"). Actually, it doesn't have any command line flags, but this is a possibility for future development.

To pass values to a script, place them after the script name on the command line. They will then be available as an array of strings in the _args variable within the script. The following example passes three values to a script.

```
./nicefile.langur "arg1" 123 "arg3"
```

5

little things

The following are some little things to address so we can go forward. Not "Could you please pick up your laundry?" or "Could you squeeze the toothpaste from the end instead of the middle?" but other little things possibly less important.

pop!

We use OpPop to clean up. Otherwise, a stack could get cluttered with data we're no longer using. Essentially, OpPop is used at the end of all statements, including "expression statements." ("Statements" do not produce a value, but "expressions" do.)

In the VM instruction loop, we have a simple pop action matched to an OpPop opcode.

```
for ip := 0; ip < len(ins); ip++ {
    op := opcode.OpCode(ins[ip])

    switch op {
    case opcode.OpPop:
        vm.pop()

    ...
```

compiling pop

You'll see OpPop very often. For the `compileNode()` method, we pass a Boolean `popAtEndOfExpression`, so that when it compiles an `*ast.ExpressionStatementNode`, it will add an OpPop instruction.

```go
func (c *Compiler) compileNode(node ast.Node, popAtEndOfExpression bool) (
    ins opcode.Instructions, err error) {

    var bSlc []byte

    switch node := node.(type) {

    ...

    case *ast.ExpressionStatementNode:
        ins, err = c.compileNode(node.Expression, true)

        if popAtEndOfExpression {
            ins = append(ins, opcode.Make(opcode.OpPop)...)
        }
```

An expression statement node would be generated by the parser to wrap a completed expression. That is, the value of the expression is not used by the end of it, thus making the expression a statement.

jump!

We often need to place precise "jumps" in instruction sets. A jump tells the VM to advance the instruction pointer, jumping past some instructions (or jumping back with OpJumpBack).

These may be unconditional from a given point (OpJump, OpJumpBack, OpJumpRelay) or conditional (OpJumpIfNotTruthy, OpJumpRelayIfNotTruthy). Note that conditional jumps pop the value they test off the stack (without an OpPop), whether the test succeeds or fails.

We also use OpJumpPlaceHolder in the compiler to fill in where we know we need a jump, but don't yet know how far. The VM will never see OpJumpPlaceHolder. We'll be using jump opcodes through much of this book, but here's a quick example.

If we go to the REPL, and type in a very simple *if* expression, we can see some jump instructions.

```
>> if true { 456 }
ByteCode Instructions
0000 True
0003 JumpIfNotTruthy 8
0008 Constant 2
0011 Jump 1
0016 Null
0017 Pop
```

As I write this, langur uses relative jumps, not absolute jumps, so rather than giving a position in the instruction set, it gives a distance.

The conditional jump, `0003 JumpIfNotTruthy 8` asks if the value at the top of the stack is "truthy" (as determined by the `object.IsTruthy()` method). If it is not, it jumps 8 bytes forward after the end of it's own instruction. Seeing that the next instruction starts at `0008`, we know that it would jump 8 more bytes to `0016` (not from `0003` to `0011`.) We also see an unconditional jump `0011 Jump 1`, which jumps 1 byte from position `0016` to `0017`. Figure 7 on the next page gives a visual representation of this.

38

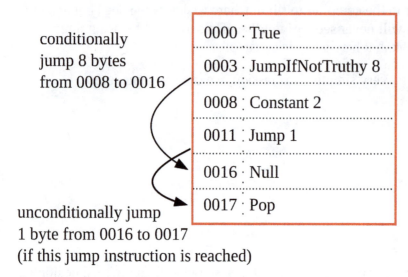

conditionally
jump 8 bytes
from 0008 to 0016

unconditionally jump
1 byte from 0016 to 0017
(if this jump instruction is reached)

figure 7: jump opcodes

scope

There are several things which can create variable scope in langur, such as ....

1. function definitions
2. generic curly braces { }
3. *for* loops
4. *catch* blocks (but not the implicit *try* section)
5. *if* expressions or *given* expressions

For some of these, we use OpExecute, which tells the VM to retrieve a constant CompiledCode object containing more VM instructions (opcodes), and execute the code. This is used for a scoped block.

Scope may also be used without an OpExecute instruction, such as with user-defined functions and with *catch* blocks (OpTryCatch).

We'll see examples of these things as we go.

short-circuiting

A short circuit means getting shocked and other bad things. No. In programming, a short circuit means that after we evaluate the left-hand operand of an operation, we determine if the right-hand operand needs to be evaluated at all. This serves a couple of purposes.

1. It can be more efficient if the right-hand operand involves a lot of calculation.
2. It can be semantically convenient knowing that a right-hand operand will not be evaluated if it would not be valid. That is, it helps us write nicer code, such as this typical example with a short-circuiting and operator....

```
if len(.s) > 0 and .s[1] == '%' { ... }
```

Short-circuiting is very useful, and langur uses it for logical operators and for an index alternate value, as we'll see.

between a compiler and a VM

The bytecode package (bytecode/bytecode.go) defines a `ByteCode struct` to hold data generated by the compiler, including a slice of strings for late-binding variable names, a slice of `Constants`, and a global `CompiledCode` object (which includes both a global instruction set and a count of global variables). After running the compiler, we pick up the constants and other values from a `ByteCode struct` that it created, and use them in initializing a new VM.

```go
type ByteCode struct {
    GlobalCode *object.CompiledCode
    Constants  []object.Object

    // global late-binding assignments for the VM ...
    // ...to fill in (opcodes already generated by Compiler)
    Late []string
}
```

We mentioned the global instruction set in discussing frames, and we're about to talk about constants.

6

constants

Constants include numbers and non-interpolated strings from literals in source code. Also, pre-compiled regexes and scoped blocks of code, including user-defined functions. A "constant" is a langur object. Objects are used to pass values around, and, as I mentioned earlier, essentially create langur's type system.

The compiler builds a slice of constants, which it will pass to the VM. Then the VM only needs an index number to be able to retrieve one. Though it is a Go slice, the VM does not change the contents or size of it. In Go, using slices is more idiomatic than using fixed-size arrays, and is easy to deal with.

In the VM, we use OpConstant to explicitly push a constant onto the stack from the constants slice. It has one operand, an index into the slice.

So, in the REPL type 7 (and hit enter), and you'll see something like this.

```
>> 7
ByteCode Instructions
0000 Constant 2
0003 Pop
```

```
ByteCode Constants
1: Number 123
2: Number 7

langur escaped result: 7
```

You see the constant 2 is the number 7 in this example. The `0000 Constant 2` pushes it onto the stack. Then, our expression is complete, so it is followed by `0003 Pop`. The last value was the 7, from the constant we pushed, so that is the result.

In the VM instruction loop, it takes just 4 lines to make OpConstant work.

```
case opcode.OpConstant:
    constIndex := opcode.ReadUInt16(ins[ip+1:])
    ip += 2
    err = vm.push(vm.constants[constIndex])
```

The code "opcode.`ReadUInt16`(`ins[ip+1:]`)" reads the operand of OpConstant and "`ip += 2`" advances the instruction pointer the distance of the operand.

Besides OpConstant, several other opcodes have operands with indices for constants, such as OpExecute and OpTryCatch have, but the VM uses those indices to retrieve constants without pushing them onto the stack.

Note: Though langur "constants" remain constant for the VM, some are altered by the compiler after being added (as you'll see later). So, they might not be "constant" during compilation.

adding constants in the compiler

We try to generate constants once, when reasonable. For example, if you use the number literal 7 twelve times in your source code, you get one constant for it, not twelve.

In compiler.go, you'll see this....

```go
func (c *Compiler) addConstant(obj object.Object) int {
    // add constants once
    idx := constantsSliceIndex(obj, c.constants)
    if idx == -1 {
        idx = len(c.constants)
        c.constants = append(c.constants, obj)
    }
    return idx
}

func constantsSliceIndex(obj object.Object, objSlc []object.Object) int {
    for i := range objSlc {
        if sameConstant(obj, objSlc[i]) {
            return i
        }
    }
    return -1
}
```

The `addConstant()` method returns the index number for a constant, which can be passed to `opcode.Make()` for an operand. The `constantsSliceIndex()` function checks if an object exists in the constants slice already (comparing via `sameConstant()`, not shown here) and returns that number to `addConstant()`, or `-1` if not present. If `addConstant()` receives `-1`, it knows it must add the constant.

As one example of using `addConstant()`, compiling a number constant looks like the following (a `case` in the `compileNode()` method).

```go
case *ast.NumberNode:
    var number *object.Number
    number, err = object.NumberFromString(node.Value, node.Base)
    ins = opcode.Make(opcode.OpConstant, c.addConstant(number))
```

Constants are relatively simple, but very important to the operation of the language.

7

retrieving non-constant values

Besides constants, there are a number of other things to specifically push onto the stack. These include global variables, local variables, non-local variables, free variables, and self references.

A local variable is one referenced in the same frame in which it is stored. A non-local is a reference to a variable stored in a different frame than it is being referenced from (not including global variables).

Free variables are discussed later when we talk about function closures, and self references are used for direct recursion of functions.

value retrieval in the VM

To retrieve things onto the stack, we use OpGetGlobal, OpGetLocal, OpGetNonLocal, OpGetFree, and OpGetSelf. We can find these and their operand widths in opcode/opcode.go.

```
OpGetGlobal:   {"GetGlobal", []int{2}},
OpGetLocal:    {"GetLocal", []int{1}},
OpGetNonLocal: {"GetNonLocal", []int{1, 1}},
OpGetBuiltIn:  {"GetBuiltIn", []int{2}},
OpGetFree:     {"GetFree", []int{1}},
OpGetSelf:     {"GetSelf", []int{}},
```

In the VM instruction loop, we find the following cases.

```
case opcode.OpGetGlobal:
    globalIndex := opcode.ReadUInt16(ins[ip+1:])
    ip += 2
    err = vm.push(vm.globalFrame.locals[globalIndex])

case opcode.OpGetLocal:
    localIndex := int(ins[ip+1])
    ip += 1
    result, err = fr.getLocal(localIndex)
    if err == nil {
        err = vm.push(result)
    }

case opcode.OpGetNonLocal:
    index := int(ins[ip+1])
    level := int(ins[ip+2])
    ip += 2

    result, err = fr.getNonLocal(index, level)
    if err == nil {
        err = vm.push(result)
    }
```

The instruction pointer (`ip` variable) is pointing to the opcode, so we use `ip+1`, `ip+2`, etc. to read in the operands. The function call `opcode.ReadUInt16(ins[ip+1:])` returns an integer, reading in the first 2 bytes from the slice it is passed (the colon being a range operator in the context of `ins[ip+1:]`). To read a single byte operand, we just read it directly (such as `int(ins[ip+2])`), using a type cast (`int(...)`) to convert it from a byte to an integer.

Having read in the operands, we advance the instruction pointer the same width as the operands (`ip += 2`). We don't advance it past the operands (will point at the last byte of the last operand), as it will be automatically advanced by 1 byte on each iteration of the instruction loop.

OpGetGlobal and OpGetLocal each have one operand, but OpGetNonLocal has two, an index and a level (or you might say frame distance).

For local value retrieval, we have the following function (in vm/frames.go).

```
func (fr *frame) getLocal(localIndex int) (
    obj object.Object, err error) {

    if fr.code.LocalBindingsCount > 0 {
        return fr.locals[localIndex], nil
    }
    return fr.base.getLocal(localIndex)
}
```

The check `fr.code.LocalBindingsCount > 0` essentially checks to see if the current frame has scope. If not, the `getLocal()` must be asking for a value in another frame.

For non-local value retrieval, we have the following.

```
func (fr *frame) getNonLocal(localIndex, count int) (
    obj object.Object, err error) {

    if count == 0 {
        return fr.locals[localIndex], nil
    }
    return fr.base.getNonLocal(localIndex, count-1)
}
```

We check the count and if not 0, decrement the count, checking the next base frame.

With getNonLocal, could we have eliminated "globals" in langur? I did not, so far, as it seemed good to keep them for at least a couple of reasons.

1. No matter how many frame levels deep you are, globals can be easily accessed by addressing them separately. This might be more efficient?

2. I've used a single byte index for locals, but a 2-byte index for globals. This means locals are limited to 256 values, but globals could include much more than that.

indexed value retrieval in the VM

Indexed retrieval is used when you have something like the following.

```
var .x = [7, 21, 35]
.x[3]
# result == 35
```

An alternate value may be used to return instead of an exception for an invalid index, such as in the following. Short-circuiting is used for the alternate value (not evaluated if not used).

```
var .x = [7, 21, 35]
.x[3; 123]    # 35
.x[7; 123]    # 123
```

The VM has the following 2 cases in its instruction loop, which call executeIndexOperation().

```
case opcode.OpIndex:
    _, err = vm.executeIndexOperation(fr, false, 0)

case opcode.OpIndexAlternate:
    shortCircuitJump := int(opcode.ReadUInt16(ins[ip+1:]))
    ip += 2

    var jumpAlt bool
    jumpAlt, err = vm.executeIndexOperation(fr, true, shortCircuitJump)
    if jumpAlt {
        ip += shortCircuitJump
    }
```

The beginning of `executeIndexOperation()` may appear a little odd, since I said that it would use short-circuiting for an alternate value. The reality is that if the alternate is very simple, such as a number or a string without interpolation, it might not use short-circuiting evaluation on it, as it could be a waste. So, if there is an alternate, but no short-circuiting, we must first pop that off the stack as it has already been evaluated.

```go
func (vm *VM) executeIndexOperation(
    fr *frame, alt bool, shortCircuitJump int) (
    jumpAlt bool, err error) {

    var alternate object.Object
    if alt && shortCircuitJump == 0 {
        // have alternate with no short-circuiting
        alternate = vm.pop()
    } else {
        // short-circuiting evaluation, or no alternate
        alternate = nil
    }
```

Then, as we'll see in discussing index opcodes and compiling them, we first pushed the indexable value to the stack ("`left`" below), then the `index`. We must pop them off the stack in the opposite order.

```go
    index := vm.pop()
    left := vm.pop()
```

Then, we evaluate these things to get a result or an error. If `alternate` is not `nil` (already known), then `object.Index()` will use that to return instead of an error for an invalid index. It would also return false for `useAlternate` since the result would already be known.

```go
    result, useAlternate, err := object.Index(left, index, alternate)
    if err != nil {
        if alt && useAlternate {
            return false, nil
        }
        return true, err
```

```
    }

    return true, vm.push(result)
}
```

If we received an index error and have an alternate value yet to evaluate and use, and `object.Index()` indicates that we should use the alternate, we then use `return false, nil` to return to the instruction loop, `false` meaning don't jump over an alternate and `nil` as we are not returning an error to the instruction loop. If we received another kind of error (unlikely), we use `return true, err` to return to the instruction loop with an error, which the instruction loop will convert to a langur exception (see the "exceptions" chapter).

If all is well, we return `true` and any error returned from `vm.push()` (likely `nil`, not an error).

The `object.Index()` method and the functions it calls don't fit into this short book, but you can view them in the object/index.go file to see how this works.

global / local value retrieval opcodes

If we declare and set a variable `.x`, then simply type `.x` in the REPL, we can see an OpGetGlobal which retrieves the value.

```
>> val .x = 21
ByteCode Instructions
0000 Constant 1
0003 SetGlobal 4
0006 Pop

>> .x
ByteCode Instructions
0000 GetGlobal 4
0003 Pop

langur escaped result: 21
```

The `GetGlobal` 4 retrieves a value set by `SetGlobal` 4. The 4 is an index into the global variables slice. Once established, an index does not change, so that a variable value may be retrieved or changed by another opcode at any point thereafter. The compiler, with its symbol tables, keeps track of indices to produce opcodes to set and retrieve a given variable by name (as discussed in the chapter on "declaration and assignment"). The VM never sees a variable name (just a number).

Opcodes for retrieving local values (those stored in the same frame as the instructions to retrieve them) look the same as for retrieving global values, except that they use OpGetLocal instead of OpGetGlobal.

non-local value retrieval opcodes

So, what's a non-local? It's not a foreigner, but a value stored on a frame higher than the frame executing the instruction to retrieve it. This being the case, an OpGetNonLocal requires another operand, the frame distance, or level, to go to find the value.

Type the following in the REPL. We have 2 scoped blocks of code. The inside block retrieves a value from the outside block.

```
>> { val .x = 7; { val .y = .x x 3 } }
ByteCode Instructions
0000 Execute 4
0003 Pop

ByteCode Constants
...
3: Code (...); LocalBindingsCount: 1
Instructions
0000 GetNonLocal 0 1
0003 Constant 2
0006 Multiply
0007 SetLocal 0
```

```
4: Code (...); LocalBindingsCount: 1
Instructions
0000 Constant 1
0003 SetLocal 0
0005 Pop
0006 Execute 3

langur escaped result: 21
```

In this example, `0000 Execute 4` executes the code in constant 4. This is the outside block of code where `.x` is set to 7. Note that the index used is 0 (`0003 SetLocal 0`). It then has instruction `0006 Execute 3` to execute the code in constant 3.

In constant 3, we have `0000 GetNonLocal 0 1`, with 2 operands, an index value and a frame level. The 0 indicates the index on the distant frame and the 1 indicates that it is 1 frame away. In that other frame, we had set `.x` using index 0, so we use the same index to retrieve it. We don't use OpGetLocal since we're in a different scoped frame, with its own local values.

The `0007 SetLocal 0` sets the value of `.y` in the inner block of code. There's no conflict between this local index 0 and the other local index 0 since they are in different frames.

indexed value retrieval opcodes

Langur allows indexing arrays, strings, and hashes by single items or by arrays. Indexing by array returns an array. Arrays and strings can also be indexed by range, or ranges may be used with indexing by array. All of the following are potentially valid for indexed value retrieval.

```
.x[1]
.x[7; 42]      # with index alternate 42
.x[2..7]
.x[[3, 4..6, 9..1]]
.y["abc"]
.y[["abc", "def"]]
.z[.x]
.z[.x[3] to 42]
```

For simplicity, and since it has no bearing on the other things we'll be looking at, we'll use a single index.

First define an indexable value in the REPL. Then, use square brackets to retrieve an indexed value from it. Note that langur uses 1-based indexing.

```
>> val .x = [4, 8, 9, 10]
   . . .
>> .x[3]
ByteCode Instructions
0000 GetGlobal 4
0003 Constant 5
0006 Index
0007 Pop

ByteCode Constants
1: Number 4
2: Number 8
3: Number 9
4: Number 10
5: Number 3

langur escaped result: 9
```

In the retrieval process, we see `0000 GetGlobal 4`, which pushes the array object represented by `.x` onto the stack. Then, we have `0003 Constant 5`. Looking at our constants, we see that this pushes the number 3 to the top of the stack. Then, `0006 Index` tells the VM to pop the index and thing to be indexed off the stack, and push the result, which in this case is the number 9, the third element of array `.x`.

While we do have the number 9 in the constants slice, that is not where the result is coming from. That 9 is from creating the original array. I suppose the REPL could do some house-keeping to eliminate things it isn't using anymore, and it might at some point, and then you wouldn't see the 9 in the constants slice as in the example.

Using an index alternate looks like the following.

```
>> .x[5; 100 x 8]
ByteCode Instructions
0000 GetGlobal 4
0003 Constant 6
0006 IndexAlternate 7
0009 Constant 7
0012 Constant 2
0015 Multiply
0016 Pop

langur escaped result: 800
```

I've spared us from viewing the constants again. The `0000 GetGlobal 4` again retrieves the value of `.x` (the array set earlier) to the stack. `0003 Constant 6` pushes the number 5 onto the stack. But then, instead of OpIndex, we have OpIndexAlternate. This includes the number of bytes to jump if an index is valid (over the alternate). In this case, it would jump 7 bytes from `0009` to `0016`, short-circuiting evaluation of the alternate value.

compiling non-constant value retrieval

Symbol tables will be discussed when we talk about assignment, but I'll mention them now. We use symbol tables to keep track of variables in the compiler, and "push" and "pop" symbol tables in the compiler as required for scope.

To know if we've defined a variable, we check for it by calling `c.symbolTable.resolve()` as shown in `compileVariableNode()` below. It will return the symbol if it can be found. The symbol contains an index number (reserved slot) into the appropriate slice of values. This index number is then used to compile both value setting and retrieval so that all the VM sees is an index number.

```
func (c *Compiler) compileVariableNode(node *ast.VariableNode) (
    ins opcode.Instructions, err error) {

    sym, cnt, ok := c.symbolTable.resolve(node.Name)
    if !ok {
        err = makeErr(node, fmt.Sprintf(
            "Undefined variable .%s", node.Name))
        return
    }

    ins, err = c.makeOpGetInstructions(node, sym, cnt)
    return
}
```

Given a defined symbol, `makeOpGetInstructions()` helps us generate the right opcodes for each symbol type.

```
func (c *Compiler) makeOpGetInstructions(
    node ast.Node, sym symbol, level int (
    ins opcode.Instructions, err error) {

    switch sym.Scope {
    case globalScope:
        return opcode.Make(opcode.OpGetGlobal, sym.Index), nil
    case localScope:
        if level == 0 {
            return opcode.Make(opcode.OpGetLocal, sym.Index), nil
        }
        return opcode.Make(opcode.OpGetNonLocal, sym.Index, level), nil
    case freeScope:
        return opcode.Make(opcode.OpGetFree, sym.Index), nil
    case selfScope:
        return c.compileSelfRef(node)
    }
    err = makeErr(node, fmt.Sprintf("Attempt to create OpGet on .%s for %s",
        sym.Name, sym.Scope))
    bug("makeOpGetInstructions", err.Error())
    return nil, err
}
```

```
func (c *Compiler) compileSelfRef(node ast.Node) (
    opcode.Instructions, error) {

    if c.symbolTable.Outer == nil {
        return nil, makeErr(node, "Cannot use self token in global scope")
    }
    return opcode.Make(opcode.OpGetSelf), nil
}
```

These call opcode.Make(), which we give the exclusive right to build opcodes to avoid some potential errors in doing so.

compiling indexed value retrieval

For indexed value retrieval, we have compileIndexExpression(), which takes an *ast.IndexNode and turns it into opcodes.

```
func (c *Compiler) compileIndexExpression(node *ast.IndexNode) (
    ins opcode.Instructions, err error) {

    var b []byte

    // Get "left" node
    b, err = c.compileNode(node.Left, true)
    if err != nil {
        return
    }
    ins = append(ins, b...)

    // Get the index
    b, err = c.compileNode(node.Index, true)
    if err != nil {
        return
    }
    ins = append(ins, b...)
```

First, we compile the thing to be indexed (the "left" operand) and the index. Pretty straightforward. The alternate index value can make it more complicated.

```go
if node.Alternate == nil {
    ins = append(ins, opcode.Make(opcode.OpIndex)...)
```

If there is no alternate, this is sufficient and will be returned as the full instruction set. That is, we have instructions to generate or retrieve the thing to be indexed, then the index itself, then an OpIndex. In the VM, with our 2 items at the top of the stack, as discussed earlier, OpIndex will tell it to pop them off and do the indexing.

If there is an alternate, we have to generate more instructions. First, we compile the alternate without adding it to the instruction set (variable `ins`), as we don't yet know where it goes.

```go
} else {
    // alternate for an invalid index
    var alt opcode.Instructions
    alt, err = c.compileNode(node.Alternate, true)
    if err != nil {
        return
    }
}
```

Having done this, we ask if short-circuiting is necessary. It will not be used for some simple cases.

```go
useShortCircuit := true
switch alt := node.Alternate.(type) {
case *ast.NumberNode, *ast.NullNode, *ast.BooleanNode:
    // no short-circuiting on some simple things
    useShortCircuit = false
case *ast.StringNode:
    // short circuit for strings that include interpolation
    useShortCircuit = len(alt.Interpolations) > 0
}
```

```
    if useShortCircuit {
        ins = append(ins, opcode.Make(
            opcode.OpIndexAlternate, len(alt))...)
        ins = append(ins, alt...)
    } else {
        ins = append(ins, alt...)
        ins = append(ins, opcode.Make(opcode.OpIndexAlternate, 0)...)
    }
}

    return
}
```

And finally, if using short-circuiting, we include the length to jump as an operand of OpIndexAlternate. If not, we use 0. Also, you'll notice that with short-circuiting, the alternate instructions are placed after the OpIndexAlternate, and without short-circuiting, they are placed before it.

Then, we return with the instructions we've built. That is all there is to compiling indexed value retrieval in langur. Setting indexed values is an entirely different process for langur.

8

operators

Operators, which are essentially built-in functions with a convenient syntax, are not difficult to code for in the compiler and VM.

For math operators, we generally try to follow the order of operations known by "PEMDAS" (Please Excuse My Dear Aunt Sally). This is a mnemonic to remember **p**arentheses, **e**xponents (powers/roots), **m**ultiplication/**d**ivision, and **a**ddition/**s**ubtraction. (According to one website, they use "BODMAS" in the UK and "BEDMAS" in Canada. It's the same.) Other than that, we generally go from left to right (left-associativity), but some operators give preference to right to left (right-associativity).

The parser has already dealt with operator precedence and associativity. It built the AST so that operations happen in a desired prescribed order when they are chained, so we won't deal much with precedence and associativity in this book. You can look at the `parseExpression()` method in parser/parser.go and also look at parser/precedence.go to see how this works.

operators in the VM

Let us look at logical operators in the VM first. We have a case in the instruction loop for logical operators that takes short-circuiting into consideration.

```
case opcode.OpLogicalAnd, opcode.OpLogicalOr,
    opcode.OpLogicalNAnd, opcode.OpLogicalNOr,
    opcode.OpLogicalNXor, opcode.OpLogicalXor:

    var left, right object.Object
    var ok bool

    // read in 2 operands
    code := int(ins[ip+1])
    ip += 1
    shortCircuitJump := int(opcode.ReadUInt16(ins[ip+1:]))
    ip += 2

    if shortCircuitJump == 0 {
        // not short-circuiting, or is second half
        right = vm.pop()
        left = vm.pop()

        result, err = object.BinaryLogicalOperation(op, left, right, code)
        if err == nil {
            err = vm.push(result)
        }

    } else {
        // have left only; haven't evaluated right yet
        // just look; don't pop
        left = vm.look()
        result, ok = object.ShortCircuitingOperation(op, left, code)
        if ok {
            // short circuit success
            // pop left now
            vm.pop()

            // jump over right evaluation
            ip += shortCircuitJump
```

```
                // push result
                err = vm.push(result)
        }
        // no result?
        // continues, starting evaluation of the right operand
    }
```

The case for comparison operators (not shown here) is almost exactly identical to this one. This first asks if short-circuiting is involved. To jump 0 bytes means no short-circuiting, because we've already evaluated the right-hand operand. This could happen because the left-hand did not short circuit after its evaluation, or because no short-circuiting was attempted in the first place (if determined unnecessary by the compiler).

If we do attempt short-circuiting, the VM first uses vm.look() to not pop the left-hand operand. We're just looking. If determined to be a successful short circuit, then we pop the value, jump the requested number of bytes in the instructions, and push the result. The VM calls object.ShortCircuitingOperation() to determine success or failure of the short circuit. We find this function in object/comparison.go. It takes the left-hand operand (now an object) and checks if it is sufficient for a result.

```go
func isDatabaseOperation(code int) bool {
    return 0 != code&opcode.OC_Database_Op
}

func ShortCircuitingOperation(op opcode.OpCode, left Object, code int) (
    result Object, haveResult bool) {

    // left only; haven't evaluated the right yet
    if isDatabaseOperation(code) {
        // database comparison; either side null, return null
        if left == NULL {
            return NULL, true
        }

        ...
```

```
    } else {
        // not a database comparison
        switch op {
        case opcode.OpLogicalAnd:
            if !IsTruthy(left) {
                return FALSE, true
            }
        case opcode.OpLogicalNAnd:
            if !IsTruthy(left) {
                return TRUE, true
            }
        case opcode.OpLogicalOr:
            if IsTruthy(left) {
                return TRUE, true
            }
        case opcode.OpLogicalNOr:
            if IsTruthy(left) {
                return FALSE, true
            }
        }
    }

    // We don't know the answer yet.
    return NO_DATA, false
}
```

operator opcodes

Some example langur operators are + (add), x (multiply), and logical operators such as and and or. Let's try simple math first, then we'll look at a short-circuiting or.

```
>> 7 x 7
ByteCode Instructions
0000 Constant 1
0003 Constant 1
0006 Multiply
0007 Pop
```

```
ByteCode Constants
1: Number 7
```

```
langur escaped result: 49
```

Here you see binary operators (which work on 2 operands) in action. We push 2 values onto the stack first, then we use the binary operator OpMultiply, which pops them off, does the math, and pushes the result. This is the typical way binary operators will work, except for short-circuiting.

What happens when we chain them together? Here's an example we saw earlier when talking about the AST (see figure 3).

```
>> 3 + 4 x 7
ByteCode Instructions
0000 Constant 2
0003 Constant 3
0006 Constant 1
0009 Multiply
0010 Add
0011 Pop
```

```
ByteCode Constants
1: Number 7
2: Number 3
3: Number 4
```

```
langur escaped result: 31
```

Expecting 49 again? Precedence. So what happens here in the opcodes? The 3 gets pushed, then the 4, then the 7. Then, with 4 and 7 at the top of the stack, we use OpMultiply (4 x 7 = 28). Now we have 3 and 28 at the top of the stack, and we use OpAdd (3 + 28 = 31).

Why would all 3 numbers get pushed first? We start the add operation by pushing the left result (3). Then, we want the right-hand result. Because of precedence, we don't add 3 and 4 and then multiply by 7, but effectively it is `3 + (4 x 7)`. The right-hand operand of OpAdd is `4 x 7`. So this has to be calculated before the addition can take place.

Try `4 x 7 + 3` and you'll see that the left-hand operand of OpAdd is calculated first. Then we push the `3`, then use OpAdd.

```
>> 4 x 7 + 3
ByteCode Instructions
0000 Constant 3
0003 Constant 1
0006 Multiply
0007 Constant 2
0010 Add
0011 Pop
```

opcodes, the stack, the VM, and RPN

If it helps, you could think of the VM as acting like a reverse Polish notation (RPN) calculator. The actions of the VM depend on the state of the stack. It is explicitly written in this manner with RPN.

Let's take the above example and write it in this notation.

```
4 7 x 3 +
```

In RPN, this means push 4, push 7, multiply, push 3, and add. Sounds like the opcodes we just looked at, doesn't it?

logical operator example with short-circuiting or operator

```
>> true or false
ByteCode Instructions
0000 True
0001 LogicalOr 0 5
0005 False
```

```
0006 LogicalOr 0 0
0010 Pop

ByteCode Constants
1: Number 7
2: Number 3
3: Number 4

langur escaped result: true
```

It is a short-circuiting or operator that causes us to see OpLogicalOr twice for one operation.[7]
The second operand of this opcode is the distance to jump (in bytes) for a short circuit.

A short-circuiting or operator stops evaluation if the left-hand is true, and a short-circuiting
and operator stops if the left-hand is false, when not used as database operators. (Database
operators, as langur has, use a different criteria, asking whether the left-hand is null.)

We see no new values in the constants slice. Just leftovers. This is because we use specific
opcodes to push true and false. It doesn't have to be that way, but it is.

OpTrue pushes true to the top of the stack. Then we have 0001 LogicalOr 0 5. Specifying
a jump of 5 bytes for a short circuit, the VM looks at the value at the top of the stack (the left-
hand value) without popping it off. It asks if this value is sufficient for a short circuit. Since it is
true in this case (and using the logical or operator), it pops the value off the stack and jumps
ahead 5 bytes. If it were not true or truthy, it would need to evaluate the right-hand operand. In
this overly-simplified case it is produced by 0005 False. Then, we have 0006 LogicalOr 0
0, specifying 0 bytes to jump for short-circuiting, meaning we have both the left- and right-
hand operands evaluated and on the stack already and this is not a short-circuiting comparison
anymore.

----

7   This is a good example in some ways. It is a bad example, since a compiler should probably
    optimize away the unneeded short-circuiting for this very simple case. :\ Actually, it could do this
    whole operation at compile-time, but let's ignore that for now. Who would write code like that,
    anyway?

compiling binary operator expressions

For this, we use `compileInfixExpression()`. You could probably call this "compile binary operator expression." (Here, we use the term "binary" to refer to an operation with 2 operands. This is not a reference to bit operations.)

We start by checking if we're dealing with a database operator. An indicator for this would be included in the first operand of the OpLogicalOr we just looked at. It was set to 0 in both cases, so was not a database operator.[8]

```go
func (c *Compiler) compileInfixExpression(node *ast.InfixExpressionNode) (
    ins opcode.Instructions, err error) {

    var left, right []byte

    code := 0
    if isDatabaseOperation(node.Operator.Code) {
        code = opcode.OC_Database_Op
    }

    left, err = c.compileNode(node.Left, true)
    if err != nil {
        return
    }
    right, err = c.compileNode(node.Right, true)
    if err != nil {
        return
    }
```

We simply compile the left and right and it's done!? Nay. Within this function, we define 4 functions to put together the opcodes, depending on the type of operation. The `plain()` function does not include a code operand for database operators and such. It also does not include short-circuiting.

---

8   This code is in theory a set of enumeration flags, though a database indicator is the only one defined as I write this.

```go
plain := func(op opcode.OpCode) (ins opcode.Instructions, err error) {
    ins = append(left, right...)
    ins = append(ins, opcode.Make(op)...)
    return ins, nil
}

nonShortCircuiting := func(op opcode.OpCode) (
        ins opcode.Instructions, err error) {
    ins = append(left, right...)
    ins = append(ins, opcode.Make(op, code, 0)...)
    return ins, nil
}

shortCircuiting := func(op opcode.OpCode) (
    ins opcode.Instructions, err error) {

    evalWithRight := opcode.Make(op, code, 0)

    // len(right)+len(evalWithRight) == opcodes to jump ...
    // ... if left is answer
    ins = append(left, opcode.Make(op, code,
        len(right)+len(evalWithRight))...)
    ins = append(ins, right...)
    // if we didn't short circuit, must evaluate here...
    ins = append(ins, evalWithRight...)

    return ins, nil
}

either := func(op opcode.OpCode) (ins opcode.Instructions, err error) {
    // either: for operations that could have ...
    // ... short-circuiting, but might not need it
    if !isDatabaseOperation(code) {
        return nonShortCircuiting(op)
    }
    return shortCircuiting(op)
}
```

Notice that the return values of these functions directly mirror the return values of `compileInfixExpression()`. Within this method, we have a `switch` statement that calls one of these functions for each `case`., returning its values directly.

You'll thank me later, as Monk would say....

```
switch node.Operator.Type {
case token.CONCATENATE:
    return plain(opcode.OpConcatenate)
case token.RANGE:
    return plain(opcode.OpRange)
case token.PLUS:
    return plain(opcode.OpAdd)
case token.MINUS:
    return plain(opcode.OpSubtract)
case token.TIMES:
    return plain(opcode.OpMultiply)
case token.DIVIDE:
    return plain(opcode.OpDivide)
case token.DIVIDEINT:
    return plain(opcode.OpIntDivide)
case token.REMAINDER:
    return plain(opcode.OpRemainder)
case token.MODULUS:
    return plain(opcode.OpModulus)
case token.EXPONENT:
    return plain(opcode.OpExponent)
case token.ROOT:
    return plain(opcode.OpRoot)

case token.EQUAL:
    return either(opcode.OpEqual)
case token.NOT_EQUAL:
    return either(opcode.OpNotEqual)
case token.GREATER_THAN:
    return either(opcode.OpGreaterThan)
case token.GT_OR_EQUAL:
    return either(opcode.OpGreaterThanOrEqual)
```

```
    case token.LESS_THAN:
        return either(opcode.OpLessThan)
    case token.LT_OR_EQUAL:
        return either(opcode.OpLessThanOrEqual)

    case token.AND:
        return shortCircuiting(opcode.OpLogicalAnd)
    case token.OR:
        return shortCircuiting(opcode.OpLogicalOr)

    case token.NAND:
        return shortCircuiting(opcode.OpLogicalNAnd)
    case token.NOR:
        return shortCircuiting(opcode.OpLogicalNOr)

    case token.XOR:
        return either(opcode.OpLogicalXor)
    case token.NXOR:
        return either(opcode.OpLogicalNXor)

    default:
        err = makeErr(node, fmt.Sprintf("unknown operator %d (%s)",
            node.Operator.Type, token.TypeDescription(node.Operator.Type)))
    }

    return
}
```

And that's it. We've compiled infix expressions, or "binary operator expressions."

What's the default for within the switch statement? It's almost always a good idea to check for an unwanted value. This will greatly benefit your coding in the future when you, I, and others inevitably make mistakes. "May all your coding be bug-free." Yeah, right. Let us move on.

9
building things

To build arrays, strings, and regexes at run-time (when necessary), we use OpArray, OpString, and OpRegex. OpArray and OpString pull a certain number of objects (specified by an operand) off the stack to use in building a new object. This only works in the VM because the compiler has generated the instructions to put all the items onto the stack ahead of the opcode used to build. We'll use arrays as the first example, since they are simpler to build than the others.

array opcodes

OpArray has one operand, the count of items on the stack to create an array object from. The VM will pop the number of items off the stack, generate the array object and push it onto the stack.

```
>> [11, 7, 21]
ByteCode Instructions
0000 Constant 1
0003 Constant 2
0006 Constant 3
0009 Array 3
0012 Pop
```

```
ByteCode Constants
1: Number 11
2: Number 7
3: Number 21

langur escaped result: [11, 7, 21]
```

The code for each element will be executed by the VM first, then it hits an OpArray opcode, pops the number of items off the stack as specified by the one operand of OpArray, builds the langur array object, and pushes it onto the stack. We could have used more complex expressions per array element and it would still have the right number of objects for the array on the stack, since each expression would produce only one value.

compiling arrays

There's not much to it. We compile each node from an *ast.ArrayNode, adding their instructions in order.

```go
func (c *Compiler) compileArrayNode(node *ast.ArrayNode) (
    ins opcode.Instructions, err error) {

    var b []byte
    for _, e := range node.Elements {
        b, err = c.compileNode(e, true)
        if err != nil {
            return
        }
        ins = append(ins, b...)
    }
    ins = append(ins, opcode.Make(opcode.OpArray, len(node.Elements))...)
    return
}
```

So, why doesn't the compiler just build the array? While that could be done for simple cases, an array could also contain variables and complex expressions that have to be evaluated before building it. So, we could use a combination of processes. That is, optimize when possible, and otherwise use the method above, using OpArray in the VM.

interpolated string opcodes

Strings with no interpolations are not built by opcode. They are constants. Interpolated strings in langur are preceded by a $ token.

Let's look at an interpolated string in the REPL.

```
>> val (.x, .y) = (78.9, "yo")
...
>> $"what's up, \.y;? a number: \.x;"
ByteCode Instructions
0000 Constant 3
0003 GetGlobal 5
0006 Constant 4
0009 GetGlobal 4
0012 String 4
0015 Pop

ByteCode Constants
 ...
3: String "what's up, "
4: String "? a number: "

langur escaped result: "what's up, yo? a number: 78.9"
```

We see four instructions preceding 0012 String 4, two string constants and two variable value retrievals. The OpString operand of 4 tells the VM to take the top 4 items off the stack and make one string out of them. But the sources aren't all strings, are they? It uses auto-stringification of the source objects. Also, if there is any formatting to be applied to interpolated values, it is done directly on those values before we reach OpString.

compiling strings

This is somewhat like compiling arrays, but more complicated.

```
func (c *Compiler) compileStringNode(node *ast.StringNode) (
    ins opcode.Instructions, err error) {

    return c.compileString(node, regex.NONE)
}
```

The string is compiled by c.compileString() rather than directly by compileStringNode() so that we can use the same code to compile interpolated literal regex pattern strings and other things.

We begin by checking for and compiling plain, non-interpolated strings. A plain string is just a constant and will not produce an OpString opcode.

```
func (c *Compiler) compileString(
    node *ast.StringNode, regexType regex.RegexType) (
    ins opcode.Instructions, err error) {

    if len(node.Interpolations) != len(node.Values)-1 {
        bug("compileString", "string value/interpolation node mismatch")
    }

    if len(node.Values) == 1 {
        // plain string (no interpolation)
        str := &object.String{Value: node.Values[0]}
        ins = opcode.Make(opcode.OpConstant, c.addConstant(str))
```

Alternatively, if we have an interpolation, we loop through the values and build opcodes for each section of the string. The lexer and parser split up the interpolation string into sections and put these into almost parallel slice fields of *ast.StringNode (Values and Interpolations). The Interpolations slice will always have 1 less item.

Let us take a quick look at the interpolation example from above.

```
$"what's up, \.y;? a number: \.x;"
```

This would produce something like what figure 8 shows. You see that there is one more item in the `Values` slice than in the `Interpolations` slice. Being a zero-length string in this case, the last value does not get added, and that's why we have `String 4` and not `String 5` in the example opcodes.

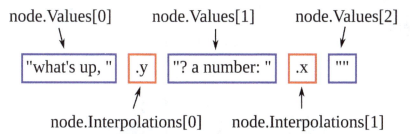

figure 8: string interpolation

We begin compiling an interpolation by looping through the range of `Values`.

```
} else {
    // interpolation
    count := 0
    for i := range node.Values {
        // add string constant
        if node.Values[i] != "" {
            str := &object.String{Value: node.Values[i]}
            ins = append(ins,
                opcode.Make(opcode.OpConstant, c.addConstant(str))...)
            count++
        }
```

You'll notice we only add non-zero-length strings and we keep a `count` going. There's no point in telling the VM to append zero-length strings.

For each value that is not the final one, there is an interpolation, so within the same loop, we add that next. We compile the interpolation and add 1 more to the `count`.

```go
if i < len(node.Values)-1 {
    // not the last string section; add interpolation value
    interp, ok := node.Interpolations[i].(*ast.InterpolatedNode)
    if !ok {
        bug("compileStringNode", fmt.Sprintf(
            "Expected interpolation node for value %d", i))
        err = makeErr(interp, fmt.Sprintf(
            "Expected interpolation node for value %d", i))
        return
    }

    interpolation, err := c.compileNode(interp.Value, false)
    if err != nil {
        return ins, err
    }
    ins = append(ins, interpolation...)
    count++
```

Then, still in the same loop, we format interpolated values, if necessary. As I write, the only formatting available was to escape characters.

```go
// escape regex meta-characters or plain string escapes?
if interp.EscMeta {
    if regexType == regex.NONE {
        // plain string
        ins = append(ins, opcode.Make(
            opcode.OpEscString, opcode.OC_Regex_None)...)
    } else if regexType == regex.RE2 {
        ins = append(ins, opcode.Make(
            opcode.OpEscString, opcode.OC_Regex_Re2)...)
    } else {
        bug("compileString", "Unknown regex type")
        err = makeErr(interp, fmt.Sprintf("Unknown regex type"))
    }
}
```

So, this will add opcodes to escape meta-characters or a plain string in an interpolated value. Just prior to this, we added instructions to generate an interpolated value, so these instructions will work directly on that value. Why does this work? What if the interpolation has many instructions (which it can)? It's not the number of instructions the interpolation has that matter, but how many items it leaves on the stack. The answer is that any one interpolation expression will only leave one object when it is finished, since all intermediate values are popped off.

The OpEscString opcode tells the VM to escape the value at the top of the stack. It will pass this to `object.EscString()`, along with a code indicating the regex type (`regex.NONE` for a plain string). This function uses auto-stringification, so that if the value is not a string already, it will become one.

After we exit the loop, adding values and interpolations, we finally generate an OpString, using `count` as the operand.

```
        ins = append(ins, opcode.Make(opcode.OpString, count)...)
    }
    return
}
```

So, when the VM hits the OpString opcode, it will know from the operand how many objects to pull off the stack, build a string object, and push it onto the stack.

interpolated regex opcodes

Just like strings, if a regex in langur does not have interpolation, it will be a constant to the VM (the regex compiled at compile-time). So, let us look at an interpolated re2 regex, preceded with a $ token. In this example, we include an indicator to tell it to escape meta-characters in the interpolated value. We start by defining a value that we will use in the interpolated regex pattern.

```
>> val .x = "^abcd*?"
...
>> $re/123+ \{\ .x}/
```

```
ByteCode Instructions
0000 Constant 2
0003 GetGlobal 4
0006 EscString 1
0008 String 2
0011 Regex 1
0013 Pop

ByteCode Constants
...
2: String "123+ "
langur escaped result: re/123+ \\^abcd\\*\\?/
```

The opening backslash after the opening curly brace in \{\ .x} is the indicator to escape meta-characters. Since the variable .x contained some re2 regex meta-characters, we see that the VM did add some backslashes to the interpolated value.

The 0000 Constant 2 retrieves the string segment "123+ " and the 0003 GetGlobal 4 retrieves the first interpolation (.x). Then 0006 EscString 1 uses an operand to indicate what type of escaping to do (1 meaning re2 meta-characters in this case, though this number could change).

Once these opcodes have executed, we have 2 strings at the top of the stack ("123+ " and the escaped interpolation value "\^abcd*\?"). 0008 String 2 pops them, makes a string, and pushes it onto the stack. Then, 0011 Regex 1 builds a regex object out of it (1 again indicating re2). I wrote langur in such a way that other regex literal types could be added. That's why we use an indicator here.

compiling regex

Here is the start of the `compileRegexNode()` function. We start by ensuring we have a string node for the pattern, then by checking the regex type and generating an operand code to match.

```go
func (c *Compiler) compileRegexNode(node *ast.RegexNode) (
    ins opcode.Instructions, err error) {

    patternNode, ok := node.Pattern.(*ast.StringNode)
    if !ok {
        return nil, makeErr(node, fmt.Sprintf(
            "Expected String Node within Regex Node"))
    }

    var code int
    if node.RegexType == regex.RE2 {
        code = opcode.OC_Regex_Re2
    } else {
        bug("compileRegexNode", "Unknown regex type")
        return nil, makeErr(node, fmt.Sprintf("Unknown regex type"))
    }
```

Then we check for interpolation, and as with compiling strings, if there is none, the compiler compiles the regex pattern right away and generates a constant from it.

```go
    if len(patternNode.Interpolations) == 0 {
        // optimize by compiling a regex pattern now, ...
        // ... rather than having the VM compile it
        var re object.Object

        re, err = object.NewRegex(patternNode.Values[0], node.RegexType)
        if err != nil {
            return
        }
        ins = opcode.Make(opcode.OpConstant, c.addConstant(re))
```

If, however, there is interpolation, we first compile the string node with c.compileString()
(which we've already looked at), then add an OpRegex.

```
    } else {
        ins, err = c.compileString(patternNode, node.RegexType)
        if err != nil {
            return
        }
        ins = append(ins, opcode.Make(opcode.OpRegex, code)...)
    }

    return
}
```

That's about all there is to compiling a regex literal in langur. If it's interpolated, the VM does
more work, and if there is none, it receives a pre-compiled regex from the compiler. The
object.NewRegex() method checks the regex type, and builds and returns a compiled regex
object or an error.

As a consequence of sometimes being pre-compiled and sometimes not, a bad regex pattern
without interpolation will cause a compile error, but with interpolation generating a bad regex
pattern, you'd get an exception in the VM.

How might you optimize some of these things? I'll leave that as homework. :]

10
declaration and assignment

Let's look at how to do variable declaration and assignment in langur. We'll look at the VM, then opcodes, then how to compile them.

Since the compiler doesn't know or care about the difference between a single assignment and multi-variable assignment, we'll deal with multi-variable assignment early on. And eventually we'll deal with decoupling assignment. Multi-variable assignment is useful not only semantically, but also makes swapping values easy and possible with no interim values (no temporary variables needed).

Multi-variable and decoupling assignments are accomplished by building opcodes. The VM knows nothing about them. It just sets one value at a time, as it is told to do so.

non-indexed assignment in the VM

Assignments will use vm.look() and not vm.pop(), since they don't pop values.

We have 3 non-index opcodes for setting variables in the VM: OpSetGlobal, OpSetLocal, and OpSetNonLocal.

```
case opcode.OpSetGlobal:
    globalIndex := opcode.ReadUInt16(ins[ip+1:])
    ip += 2
    // look() doesn't pop, so that assignment is an expression
    vm.globalFrame.locals[globalIndex] = vm.look()
```

If we have OpSetGlobal, the VM handles it directly, as it is simply an index into the globals slice. Since this slice is on the global frame, we use `vm.globalFrame.locals[globalIndex]` to set or retrieve this value.

If we have OpSetLocal or OpSetNonLocal, we use methods defined for frames.

```
case opcode.OpSetLocal:
    localIndex := int(ins[ip+1])
    ip += 1
    // look() doesn't pop, so that assignment is an expression
    fr.setLocal(localIndex, vm.look())

case opcode.OpSetNonLocal:
    index := int(ins[ip+1])
    level := int(ins[ip+2])
    ip += 2

    // look() doesn't pop, so that assignment is an expression
    fr.setNonLocal(index, level, vm.look())
```

In vm/frames.go, we see the frame methods used for these.

```
func (fr *frame) setLocal(localIndex int, setTo object.Object) {
    if fr.code.LocalBindingsCount > 0 {
        fr.locals[localIndex] = setTo
    } else {
        fr.base.setLocal(localIndex, setTo)
    }
}
```

```
func (fr *frame) setNonLocal(localIndex, count int, setTo object.Object) {
    if count == 0 {
        fr.locals[localIndex] = setTo
    } else {
        fr.base.setNonLocal(localIndex, count-1, setTo)
    }
}
```

These operate the same as the getLocal() and getNonLocal() methods (as discussed in the chapter on "retrieving non-constant values"), but to set values instead of retrieving them.

indexed assignment in the VM

For indexed assignment, it gets more complicated, but it's relatively simple in the VM. It leaves some complications to the object package. The object to use as an index is first popped off the stack (was pushed last, as set up by the compiler). Then, we just look at and don't remove the value we're setting a variable to. The variable, of course, is not on the stack, but is referenced by the index operand following the opcode.

```
case opcode.OpSetGlobalIndexedValue:
    globalIndex := opcode.ReadUInt16(ins[ip+1:])
    ip += 2

    objIdx := vm.pop()
    setTo := vm.look()

    var setObj object.Object
    setObj, err = object.SetIndex(
        vm.globalFrame.locals[globalIndex],
        objIdx, setTo)

    if err != nil {
        return
    }
    vm.globalFrame.locals[globalIndex] = setObj
```

Again, for setting global variables, the VM handles it more directly than for locals. It first makes a call to object.SetIndex(), passing it three objects (the object to set an index on, the indexing object, and the value object). If all is well, we set the index of the variable to the result received.

The OpSetLocalIndexedValue and OpSetNonLocalIndexedValue use frame methods, as OpSetLocalValue and OpSetNonLocalValue do.

```
case opcode.OpSetLocalIndexedValue:
    localIndex := int(ins[ip+1])
    ip += 1

    objIdx := vm.pop()
    setTo := vm.look()

    err = fr.setLocalIndexedValue(localIndex, objIdx, setTo)

case opcode.OpSetNonLocalIndexedValue:
    index := int(ins[ip+1])
    level := int(ins[ip+2])
    ip += 2

    objIdx := vm.pop()
    setTo := vm.look()
    err = fr.setNonLocalIndexedValue(index, level, objIdx, setTo)
```

The called frame methods look about the same as the others, but they call object.SetIndex() to set up an object just as OpSetGlobalIndexedValue does. The function object.SetIndex() is simpler than object.Index(), because it does not have as many options as object.Index(). That is, you can use an array or range as an index for value retrieval, but you can't, so far, use an array or range as an index for assigning to a variable. This is on a long list of possibilities for future development.

So far, there are 3 cases in `object.SetIndex()`. We could set an indexed value on an array, a hash, or a string. For brevity, I'll only show one of them here. You can view the entire function in object/index.go.

```go
func SetIndex(obj, index, setTo Object) (Object, error) {
    // assumes mutability of an object (checked elsewhere)
    switch o := obj.(type) {
    case *Array:
        n, ok := NumberToInt(index)
        if !ok {
            return obj, fmt.Errorf(
                "Cannot set array value from invalid index (non-integer)")
        }
        if n < 1 || n > len(o.Elements) {
            return obj, fmt.Errorf(
                "Cannot set array value from invalid index")
        }

        // Since we don't know how many references ...
        // ... there are to the array object we're changing, ...
        // ... we make a new one.
        o = o.CopyRefs().(*Array)

        // n-1 as langur uses 1-based indexing
        o.Elements[n-1] = setTo
        return o, nil

    ...

    }
    return obj, fmt.Errorf(
        "Cannot set index value of type %s",
        TypeDescription(obj.Type()))
}
```

This makes a copy of a langur array object before setting an index. Really, it copies the references to a new langur array object. This is because there could be other references to this array and we just don't know. Also, langur does not have *lvalues* and *rvalues*. Other languages and systems may do things differently.

assignment opcodes

For langur, there are some differences between declaration assignments and non-declaration assignments (to existing variables) in the compiler, but not to the VM. In the example below, we first declare and assign a variable .x. You can see that in the reassignment, the opcodes are identical to the declaration assignment that precedes it. This is because declaration is handled entirely by the compiler. We will see more about this shortly.

```
>> var .x = 7
ByteCode Instructions
0000 Constant 2
0003 SetGlobal 4
0006 Pop

>> .x = 7
ByteCode Instructions
0000 Constant 2
0003 SetGlobal 4
0006 Pop
```

We learned earlier that OpConstant pushes a constant onto the stack. In this case, our constant is the number 7. Then, we see `0003 SetGlobal 4`. This has one operand, a global variable index value.

Since we're at the end of the statement, we see `0006 Pop`. The assignment itself does not add this OpPop. Assignment in langur is an expression. This means that the last value assigned is not popped off the stack by the assignment. (In multi-variable assignment, all but the last value are popped off by the assignment.)

For multi-variable assignment, we essentially do the same thing as for single assignment, but we push the values onto the stack in reverse order before setting variables and popping them off.

```
>> var (.x, .y) = (7, 14)
ByteCode Instructions
0000 Constant 2
0003 Constant 3
0006 SetGlobal 4
0009 Pop
0010 SetGlobal 5
0013 Pop

ByteCode Constants
...
2: Number 14
3: Number 7
langur escaped result: 14
```

`0000 Constant 2` pushes the number 14 (the last value pushed first), then `0003 Constant 3` pushes the number 7.

Then, `0006 SetGlobal 4` sets .x to the top value on the stack (7). Then, we pop that value, and set .y to 14 (0010 SetGlobal 5). After this expression, the statement is over, so we pop the last value.

Here's a contrived, but simple, example of assignment as an expression. After we assign to .x, we check if the value is over 21. This is only possible because we didn't pop the value immediately after assignment.

```
>> (.x = .y) > 21
ByteCode Instructions
0000 GetGlobal 5
0003 SetGlobal 4
0006 Constant 3
0009 GreaterThan 0 0
```

```
0013 Pop
```

The `0000 GetGlobal 5` retrieves `.y` and `0003 SetGlobal 4` sets `.x`. Then, `0006 Constant 3` retrieves `21`. Now, we have the values of `.x` and `21` at the top of the stack. Then `0009 GreaterThan 0 0` pops both values and compares them, pushing the result (`true` or `false`). `0013 Pop` will pop this Boolean off the stack since the expression is over.

For non-global variables, it can be more complicated. We have OpSetLocal for setting a variable within a local frame and OpSetNonLocal for setting a variable from a higher frame (when allowed), since each scoped frame carries its own locals. (Some frames, such as the *try* frame of *try/catch*, don't have scope and carry no locals.)

```
>> { val .x = 21 }
ByteCode Instructions
0000 Execute 3
0003 Pop

ByteCode Constants
1: Number 7
2: Number 21
3: Code (...); LocalBindingsCount: 1
Instructions
0000 Constant 2
0003 SetLocal 0
```

So, where is the assignment in these opcodes? It's inside the scoped block, referenced by `0000 Execute 3` above. We can see constant 3 is a block of code that contains an assignment (`0003 SetLocal 0`). There is no pop instruction at the end of the frame because we want to keep the last value that was generated in the frame.

Let's take a quick look at setting a non-local. I added `var .y;` below just to create more scope so we can see this.

```
>> { var .x; { var .y; .x = 49 } }
ByteCode Instructions
0000 Execute 3
0003 Pop

ByteCode Constants
1: Number 49
2: Code (...); LocalBindingsCount: 1
Instructions
0000 Null
0001 SetLocal 0
0003 Pop
0004 Constant 1
0007 SetNonLocal 0 1

3: Code (...); LocalBindingsCount: 1
Instructions
0000 Null
0001 SetLocal 0
0003 Pop
0004 Execute 2
```

Here, we have two scope blocks. In the first, we declare a mutable variable .x (see constant 3), which is implicitly set to null because we didn't assign it to anything. We see the same thing with .y in constant 2. But then, we have 0007 SetNonLocal 0 1, which sets .x from another frame. This opcode (OpSetNonLocal) has 2 operands (index and level). In this case, we're 1 frame out, so the level is 1.

Note that OpSetNonLocal and OpGetNonLocal might be used where scope is not involved, as they apply to frames in the VM (blocks of code by the compiler), which are used for more than scope.

decoupling assignment

What is decoupling assignment? When we have one node from the parser on the right, but multiple nodes on the left to assign to, this means we need to index into the value at the right to find out what to assign.

For an example, here's a langur function I use as part of the process to convert Unicode files into Go source code.

```
val .cpOrRangeString = f(.cpOrRange) {
    if val (.start, .end) =
        submatch($re/(\.cpregex;)\\.\\.(\.cpregex;)/, .cpOrRange) {

        $"\t\tcpset.Range{Start: 0x\.start;, End: 0x\.end;},\n"
    } else {
        $"\t\trune(0x\.cpOrRange;),\n"
    }
}
```

A decoupling assignment returns a Boolean, rather than any value assigned. This allows us to use it within an if expression test as shown above. The langur `submatch()` function will return an array of submatches found, or an empty array. If the array produced from a decoupling right-hand expression does not contain enough elements to set the values on the left, the assignment will fail, returning `false`. (If it is a hash containing enough elements, but not the right number keys, it will throw an exception.)

(Note that `submatch()` is not a progressive, or "global" function. The `submatches()` function is. Progressive regex functions in langur, except for `split()` and `replace()`, use a plural form for their names.)

We'll return to decoupling assignment shortly.

compiling declarations and assignments

The compiler uses symbol tables to keep a check on what has been declared so far and whether it was declared as mutable. The VM knows nothing of the compiler's symbol tables.

Instructions and binding counts are placed into CompiledCode objects (see object/functions.go). The VM will use frames to execute these blocks of code as needed. In allocating a frame, the VM sees the count from the CompiledCode object and allocates enough space for its local bindings. The indices on opcodes, as defined by the compiler, point to these reserved spaces. So, to the langur VM, a variable is nothing more than an index into a frame's slice of locals.

symbol tables

Let's take a quick look at symbol tables so we can understand something of the declarations to follow. Looking at the file compiler/symbol_table.go, we have the following definitions.

```
type symbol struct {
        Name       string
        Scope      symbolScope
        Index      int
        mutable    bool
}

type SymbolTable struct {
        Outer            *SymbolTable
        store            map[string]symbol
        definitionCount  int
        FreeSymbols      []symbol
        isFunction       bool
}
```

The symbol table's `store` field contains a Go map of strings to symbols. The strings are the names of variables (which are also set on the symbols themselves). When we declare a variable in the compiler, we "define" it in a symbol table. When we try to use or reassign a variable in the compiler, we must "resolve" it from a symbol table for verification and to get its index (and frame level, if non-local and not a "free" variable). We use as many symbol tables as necessary, each defining a new variable scope.

Whenever we use c.pushVariableScope() in the compiler, we get a new symbol table, and its Outer field points to the symbol table we were using before we pushed scope. When we use c.popVariableScope(), the symbol table in use is discarded, and we return to using the previous one. This helps us keep track of scope in regards to variable names defined, to count locals, and to establish unique index numbers for each variable. The indices will be important when we generate opcodes which refer to them, as they must be consistent per variable name. We'll save the locals counts in CompiledCode objects so the VM knows how much space to allocate for them before it executes the opcodes in a frame.

To declare, or "define" a symbol, the compiler calls defineUserVariable() or defineSystemVariable(), either of which will call defineSymbol().

```go
func (st *SymbolTable) defineUserVariable(name string, mutable bool) (
    sym symbol, err error) {

    if name[0] == '_' {
        err = fmt.Errorf(
            "User-defined variable names cannot start with underscore")
        return
    }
    return st.defineSymbol(name, mutable)
}

func (st *SymbolTable) defineSystemVariable(name string, mutable bool) (
    sym symbol, err error) {

    if name[0] != '_' {
        bug("defineSystemVariable",
            fmt.Sprintf("System variable name %q invalid", name))
        err = fmt.Errorf("System variable names start with underscore")
        return
    }
```

```go
    return st.defineSymbol(name, mutable)
}

func (st *SymbolTable) defineSymbol(name string, mutable bool) (
    symbol, error) {

    // first, check if it is already defined in this scope
    sym, ok := st.store[name]
    if ok {
        return sym, fmt.Errorf(
            "Cannot declare %s already declared within scope",
            name)
    }

    sym = symbol{
        Name:     name,
        Index:    st.definitionCount,
        mutable:  mutable,
    }

    if st.Outer == nil {
        sym.Scope = globalScope
    } else {
        sym.Scope = localScope
    }

    st.store[name] = sym
    st.definitionCount++

    return sym, nil
}
```

The first part of `defineSymbol()` checks to see if the variable is already defined in the symbol table. If so, we have a double declaration, which is not allowed.

If it is not already defined in scope, we create a new symbol with an index number the same as the previous definition count. (If you have 4 symbols already defined, they will be indexed by the VM from 0 to 3, and a new one will be indexed at 4. The definition count will be increased to 5 by `st.definitionCount++`, allowing indexing from 0 to 4 in the VM). We add this to our existing store of symbols within the symbol table (`st.store[name] = sym`).

To resolve a variable, the compiler calls `resolve()`, which calls `resolveSymbol()` with frame level 0, and `resolveSymbol()` may call itself, checking the `Outer` field in the symbol table to check for non-locals, which will be at other frame levels in the VM.

```go
func (st *SymbolTable) resolveSymbol(name string, fromLevel int) (
    sym symbol, level int, ok bool) {

    level = fromLevel

    sym, ok = st.store[name]

    if !ok && st.Outer != nil {
        // not found in current symbol table
        // check outer symbol table
        sym, level, ok = st.Outer.resolveSymbol(name, fromLevel+1)

        if ok && st.isFunction {
            // resolves from beyond function border
            // define a "free" variable for this scope
            sym = st.defineFree(sym)
        }
    }

    return
}
```

The level returned from `resolveSymbol()` tells us exactly what level to use when retrieving or setting the variable (if it is mutable). You'll see this in the `makeOpSetInstructions()` function shortly.

You'll see in the chapter on "user-defined functions" that "free" symbols are values outside of a function closed over at the point of a function's definition. So, free symbols are defined by resolveSymbol().

```go
func (st *SymbolTable) defineFree(original symbol) symbol {
    st.FreeSymbols = append(st.FreeSymbols, original)

    sym := symbol{
        Name:     original.Name,
        Index:    len(st.FreeSymbols) - 1,
        Scope:    freeScope,
        mutable:  false,
    }

    st.store[original.Name] = sym
    return sym
}
```

When we define a free symbol, we do a couple of things. We add it to the FreeSymbols slice, so they can all be picked up by compileFunctionNode(), for building opcodes to put them onto the stack prior to an OpClosure (see "closures" in the "user-defined functions" chapter). We also add it to the symbol table store so the next call to resolveSymbol() will resolve it.

compiler declaration and assignment functions

Enough of symbol tables for now. Please load the file compiler/assign.go in your IDE. In assign.go, there are 6 major functions we'll be looking at (some involving decoupling assignments).

helper methods for compiling assignment

We'll start with makeOpSetInstructions(). This is not used for compiling an indexed assignment or a decoupling assignment.

```
func (c *Compiler) makeOpSetInstructions(
    node ast.Node, sym symbol, level int) (ins opcode.Instructions) {

    if sym.Scope == globalScope {
        ins = opcode.Make(opcode.OpSetGlobal, sym.Index)

    } else if sym.Scope == localScope {
        if level == 0 {
            ins = opcode.Make(opcode.OpSetLocal, sym.Index)
        } else {
            ins = opcode.Make(opcode.OpSetNonLocal, sym.Index, level)
        }

    } else {
        err := makeErr(node, fmt.Sprintf(
            "Attempt to create instructions in scope %s unaccounted for",
            sym.Name, sym.Scope))
        bug("makeOpSetInstructions", err.Error())
    }
    return
}
```

This function is called by `compileDeclarationAndAssignments()` or by `compileAssignment()`, which we will see shortly. It generates opcodes to set a global or local (or "non-local") value only. You'll notice the absence of some of the scope types used in `makeOpGetInstructions()`, since the other scope types are not settable.

The "non-local" designation is only for the VM. To the compiler, it is a variable with "local" scope and a "level" (distance) greater than 0 (local in another symbol table for the compiler, another frame for the VM). Thus, there is no "non-local" scope in the compiler.

Very similar is `makeOpSetIndexInstructions()`. First, it compiles an index value.

```
func (c *Compiler) makeOpSetIndexInstructions(
    node ast.Node, sym symbol, level int, index ast.Node) (
    ins opcode.Instructions, err error) {

    ins, err = c.compileNode(index, false)
    if err != nil {
        return
    }
}
```

After that, it looks almost the same as makeOpSetInstructions(), but for the different opcodes used (OpSetGlobalIndexedValue, OpSetLocalIndexedValue, and OpSetNonLocalIndexedValue). When the VM sees these, it knows it has to pop and use an index value first (which the instructions here would have pushed to the stack) and calls a function in the object package to set the indexed value within an object.

compiling declaration assignments

Declarations are made with val or var tokens in langur, such as in the following examples.

```
val .x = 123    # immutable value .x
var .y = 789    # mutable variable .y
```

Compiling mutable or immutable variable declarations is essentially the same in langur, with their mutability noted in the symbol table. The langur VM assumes mutability, and thus it is the compiler's responsibility to ensure that an "immutable" value is not set a second time once declared. A "strongly" typed language might deal with this differently, but langur is a "scripting" language.

Someone may point out that langur's "immutable" variables aren't immutable. For langur 0.5, this really means not mutable by the user. You'll see this if you look at *for in* and *for of* loops. The loop control variables are protected (not mutable by the user, but they do change).

Compiling a single declaration and assignment or multiple is the same, and the parser packages it the same way. Multi-variable declaration and assignment looks like the following.

```
val (.x, .y) = (7, 14)
# .x set immutably to 7 and .y to 14
```

We start with a declaration node. Within that, we need an assignment node.

```
func (c *Compiler) compileDeclarationAndAssignments(
    decl *ast.DeclarationNode) (
    ins opcode.Instructions, err error) {

    assign, ok := decl.Assignment.(*ast.AssignmentNode)
    if !ok {
        // parser failed
        bug("compileDeclarationAndAssignments",
            "Expected *ast.AssignmentNode in *ast.DeclarationNode")
        err = fmt.Errorf("Expected assignment node in declaration node")
        return
    }
```

A declaration, if it is mutable (using the `var` token), does not require assignments. Thus, `assign.Values == nil` as shown below is acceptable. (The parser has ensured that immutable declarations (using the `val` token) are paired with assignments.)

If the number of assignment values is not 0, we check that the number of values received matches the number of identifiers.

```
if assign.Values == nil || len(assign.Values) == len(assign.Identifiers) {
    // Compile values first (must be on the stack), ...
    // ... then setting instructions.
    var temp opcode.Instructions
    // push values in reverse order
    for i := len(assign.Values) - 1; i > -1; i-- {
        temp, err = c.compileNode(assign.Values[i], false)
        if err != nil {
            return
        }
        ins = append(ins, temp...)
    }
```

We push the values to assign in reverse order, since they are put onto a stack and not a queue. That is, when we pop the first one off the stack, it is paired with the first variable used, and when we get to the last one, it is paired with the last variable used (but not popped). If it is a single assignment, the only value is the last value, so the same method works just fine.

In our instructions, having pushed the values we want to set, we then need instructions to set the variables and to pop all but the last value. Before we actually create those instructions, we attempt to add them to our current symbol table. If already present, we will get an error and compiling will fail. Remember, symbol tables used in the compiler help us define scope for the VM. A variable name can be re-declared, but not in the same symbol table (and so, not in the same scope).

```go
for i, id := range assign.Identifiers {
    variable, ok := id.(*ast.VariableNode)
    if !ok {
        bug("compileDeclarationAndAssignments", fmt.Sprintf(
            "Wrong type in Declaration Assignment: %T", id))
    }

    var sym symbol
    if variable.System {
        sym, err = c.symbolTable.defineSystemVariable(
            variable.Name, decl.Mutable)
    } else {
        sym, err = c.symbolTable.defineUserVariable(
            variable.Name, decl.Mutable)
    }
    if err != nil {
        err = makeErr(assign, err.Error())
        return
    }

    ins = append(ins, c.makeOpSetInstructions(assign, sym, 0)...)
```

```
    // pop all but the last one
    if i < len(assign.Identifiers)-1 {
        ins = append(ins, opcode.Make(opcode.OpPop)...)
    }
}
```

Once we have a symbol to use, we call `makeOpSetInstructions()` (which we just looked at) to create the instructions. Then, if not the last assignment in the node, we add a pop instruction.

Then there's the rest....

```
    } else if len(assign.Values) == 1 {
        ins, err = c.compileDecouplingDeclarationAssignment(
            assign, decl.Mutable)

    } else {
        // parser should have caught this...
        bug("compileDeclarationAndAssignments",
            "Identifier/value mismatch in Declaration Assignment node")
    }

    return
}
```

If we have multiple variables and one value node to assign from, it is a decoupling assignment and calls another function for that. That is another animal, so to speak, which we will get to shortly.

compiling non-declaration assignment

Compiling assignment apart from declaration is somewhat different, in that, instead of defining symbols, we retrieve symbols already defined to determine how to set them. Simple assignments in langur code look like the following and require mutable variables that are already declared. If not in the current scope, those declared mutable in a higher scope may be set (but not beyond a function boundary).

```
.x = 123
(.y, .z) = (21, 49)
.a[1] = 77
```

Again, it doesn't matter if we're compiling one assignment or a multi-variable assignment. The process is the same.

We start `compileAssignment()` by asking if the number of variables to assign to is the same as the number of values. If so, we generate opcodes to push the values in reverse order, just as with compiling declarations with assignments.

```go
func (c *Compiler) compileAssignment(node *ast.AssignmentNode) (
    ins opcode.Instructions, err error) {

    if len(node.Values) == len(node.Identifiers) {
        // push values in reverse order
        var temp opcode.Instructions
        for i := len(node.Values) - 1; i > -1; i-- {
            temp, err = c.compileNode(node.Values[i], false)
            if err != nil {
                return
            }
            ins = append(ins, temp...)
        }
    }
```

Then, we loop through the Identifiers. For each one, we ask if it's a variable or index node. (We didn't allow index nodes on declarations, as that would make no sense.)

```go
var variable *ast.VariableNode
var index ast.Node
for i, id := range node.Identifiers {
    switch n := id.(type) {
    case *ast.VariableNode:
        variable = n
        index = nil
```

```
case *ast.IndexNode:
    // .x[1] = ...
    variable = n.Left.(*ast.VariableNode)
    index = n.Index

default:
    bug("compileAssignment", fmt.Sprintf(
        "Invalid node type for assignment identifier: %T", n))
}
```

Having determined these things and saving pointers to a `variable` node and an `index` node to use, and still in the loop of `node.Identifiers`, we attempt to resolve the variable and see if it can be set in this way or not.

```
name := variable.Name
sym, cnt, ok := c.symbolTable.resolve(name)
if !ok {
    err = makeErr(node, fmt.Sprintf(
        "Unable to resolve variable .%s for assignment", name))
    return
}

if !sym.mutable && !node.SystemAssignment {
    if variable.System {
        err = makeErr(node, fmt.Sprintf(
            "Cannot assign to system variable %s (not mutable by user)",
            name))
    } else {
        err = makeErr(node, fmt.Sprintf(
            "Cannot assign to immutable .%s", name))
    }
    return
}
```

Having determined the variable's eligibility to be set and having the information to do so, we use `makeOpSetInstructions()` or `makeOpSetIndexInstructions()` to generate instructions to set one value.

```
    if index == nil {
        ins = append(ins, c.makeOpSetInstructions(node, sym, cnt)...)
    } else {
        var temp opcode.Instructions
        temp, err = c.makeOpSetIndexInstructions(node, sym, cnt, index)
        if err != nil {
            return
        }
        ins = append(ins, temp...)
    }

    // pop all but the last one
    if i < len(node.Identifiers)-1 {
        ins = append(ins, opcode.Make(opcode.OpPop)...)
    }
}
```

If not the last one, we generate an instruction to pop its value off the stack. Finally, having checked if the number of values and identifiers are the same, failing that, we check whether the number of values is 1.

```
    } else if len(node.Values) == 1 {
        ins, err = c.compileDecouplingAssignment(node)

    } else {
        bug("compileAssignment",
            "Identifier/value count mismatch in Assignment node")
    }

    return
}
```

We delegate decoupling assignment to compileDecouplingAssignment(). And, if none of the above are true, we have a bug, since the parser has given the compiler bad information.

compiling decoupling declaration and assignment

The `compileDecouplingDeclarationAssignment()` function is not long itself, but relies on extra node creation from the AST, which we'll see in a moment.

First, we create an internal local variable node to set our right-hand value to before creating instructions to attempt to check the length and retrieve indexed values from it. This is a not a conflict with any other variable, because the decoupling assignment will receive its own scope for this purpose.

```
func (c *Compiler) compileDecouplingDeclarationAssignment(
    node *ast.AssignmentNode, mutable bool) (
    ins opcode.Instructions, err error) {

    tempCompositeResultVarNode :=
        &ast.VariableNode{Name: "_Decouple_", System: true}

    setResultsNodes := []ast.Node{}
    setNonResultsNodes := []ast.Node{}
```

Not knowing the outcome ahead of time, we need two slices of nodes, one for success and one for failure. We're going back to the AST here and will be creating our own nodes for the compiler to do more with.

Now, we loop through the identifiers and generate something for `setResultsNodes` and `setNonResultsNodes` for each identifier. We set each of `setNonResultsNodes` to a langur `null` object to ensure we don't get a Go exception in the VM by trying to access a variable that is actually set to `nil` in Go. For no-op nodes (indicated with an underscore in a decoupling variable list), there's nothing to set, so we skip these index numbers.

```
for i, id := range node.Identifiers {
    switch variable := id.(type) {
    case *ast.NoOpNode:
        // skip index number
        continue

    case *ast.VariableNode:
        value := &ast.IndexNode{
            Left:  tempCompositeResultVarNode,
            Index: &ast.NumberNode{Value: str.IntToStr(i+1, 10)},
        }
        setResultsNodes = append(setResultsNodes,
            ast.MakeAssignmentStatement(id, value, true))
        setNonResultsNodes = append(setNonResultsNodes,
            ast.MakeAssignmentStatement(id, ast.NoValue, true))

        _, err = c.symbolTable.defineUserVariable(
                variable.Name, mutable)

        if err != nil {
            err = makeErr(node, err.Error())
            return
        }

    default:
        bug("compileDecouplingDeclarationAssignment",
            fmt.Sprintf("Bad node for decl. assign id: %T", id))
    }
}
```

Being a declaration assignment, we attempt to define the variables as well. You'll note that we haven't pushed variable scope in the compiler, as this would create a problem here, though the decoupling assignment itself will have scope. We don't want our new definitions to have new scope, or they would be gone after the decoupling assignment, and utterly useless. You may have noticed another function in the AST (ast.MakeDeclarationAssignmentStatement()) which we don't use here. We need the variables defined in the current symbol table, not the symbol table that the temporary decoupling variable will be defined in and confined to.

The decoupling langur variable we create with `tempCompositeResultVarNode` is not yet defined in a symbol table. We've only generated an AST node for it. It will be defined when it is finally compiled inside a scoped block node.

We generate some more tree leaves and compile them.

```
newAst := ast.MakeDecouplingAssignment(
    node, tempCompositeResultVarNode,
    setResultsNodes, setNonResultsNodes)

ins, err = c.compileNode(newAst, false)
return
}
```

We use `false` to tell the compiler not to add a pop instruction at the end if it would, as we'll need the last value in the VM (a langur `true` or `false` object).

So, what's this `ast.MakeDecouplingAssignment()`? I said we weren't getting into the parser in this book, and we aren't. Generally, we let the parser generate the AST, but here we're making some of our own. As I write, this function is contained in the file langur/ast/build.go.

Here it is if you want to look at it, or if you don't. :|

```
func MakeDecouplingAssignment(
    assign *AssignmentNode,
    tempCompositeResultVarNode Node,
    setResultsNodes, setNonResultsNodes []Node) Node {

    return &BlockNode{
        Token:     assign.TokenInfo(),
        HasScope: true,
        Statements: []Node{
            // first evaluate and assign result ...
            // ... to a temporary system variable
            MakeDeclarationAssignmentStatement(
                tempCompositeResultVarNode,
                assign.Values[0], true, false),
```

```
&IfNode{
    Token: assign.TokenInfo(),
    TestsAndActions: []TestDo{
        // if len(decouple) < len(Identifiers) {} else {}
        {
            // check if enough elements available
            Test: &InfixExpressionNode{
                Left: &CallNode{
                    Function: &BuiltInNode{Name: "len"},
                    Args: []Node{tempCompositeResultVarNode},
                },

                Operator: token.Token{
                    Type: token.LESS_THAN, Literal: "(<)"},

                Right:     &NumberNode{Value:
                    str.IntToStr(len(assign.Identifiers), 10),
                },
            },
            // not enough elements
            Do: &BlockNode{
                Statements: append(setNonResultsNodes,
                    &BooleanNode{Value: false})},
                    // return false for failure
        },

        // } else {
        {
            Test: nil, // no test on else
            Do: &BlockNode{
                Statements: append(setResultsNodes,
                    &BooleanNode{Value: true})},
                    // return true for success
        },
    },
    },
    },
    }
}
```

Note that the BlockNode we build has set "HasScope: `true`". When compiled, this gives us the scope we need for the internal decoupling variable, with `MakeDeclarationAssignmentStatement()` generating the assignment to it.

We also see the `setResultsNodes` and `setNonResultsNodes` node slices put to use in this new AST construction. We append *true* or *false* nodes to each to give us our success or failure Boolean.

compiling non-declaration decoupling assignment

The `compileDecouplingAssignment()` is actually shorter and easier as it does not have to define or resolve variables (directly). It does not have to resolve them directly, because the compiler will catch any errors when it compiles the new AST leaves we build.

It starts the same as `compileDecouplingDeclarationAssignment()`.

```
func (c *Compiler) compileDecouplingAssignment(node *ast.AssignmentNode) (
    ins opcode.Instructions, err error) {

    tempCompositeResultVarNode :=
        &ast.VariableNode{Name: "_Decouple_", System: true}

    setResultsNodes := []ast.Node{}
```

We don't need a node for each failed assignment in this case, as the variables used have already been declared.

```go
for i, id := range node.Identifiers {
    switch id.(type) {
    case *ast.NoOpNode:
        // skip number
        continue

    case *ast.VariableNode, *ast.IndexNode:
        value := &ast.IndexNode{
            Left:  tempCompositeResultVarNode,
            Index: &ast.NumberNode{Value: str.IntToStr(i+1, 10)},
        }
        setResultsNodes = append(setResultsNodes,
            ast.MakeAssignmentStatement(id, value, true))

    default:
        bug("compileAssignmentNode",
            fmt.Sprintf(
                "Invalid node type for assignment identifier: %T", id))
    }
}
```

You'll notice something else. In this non-declaration assignment, we allow setting indexed values as well. We don't do the work for assignment at this point. The compiler will handle it from the new tree nodes we generate.

```go
newAst := ast.MakeDecouplingAssignment(
    node, tempCompositeResultVarNode, setResultsNodes, nil)

ins, err = c.compileNode(newAst, false)
return
}
```

We call ast.MakeDecouplingAssignment() from this function as well, but use nil for the setNonResultsNodes as we have none. We'll still get a true or false result without declaration. We just don't set anything if it fails. And that is it.

11
user-defined functions

A user-defined function is declared like the following. In this example, it is assigned to immutable value `.factorial`.

```
val .factorial = f(.x) { if .x < 2 { 1 } else { .x x self(.x - 1) } }
```

Using a shortened form *if* expression, implied parameters, and the function body being a single expression, we could write...

```
val .factorial = f if(.x < 2: 1; .x x self(.x - 1))
```

Langur functions do not have to be assigned. In fact, they are often useful as anonymous functions sent to built-in functions, such as `map()` and `fold()`.

```
map(f .x x 2, .somearray)
# This will create a new array, doubling the value of each element

fold(f .x + .y, .somearray)
# This will create a summary of values from an array
```

calling functions in the VM

A function call is made in the instruction loop via OpCall. This could be a built-in or a user-defined function.

```
case opcode.OpCall:
    argCount := int(ins[ip+1])
    ip += 1

    result, err = vm.executeFunctionCall(fr, argCount)
    if err == nil {
        err = vm.push(result)
    }
```

In the vm.executeFunctionCall() method, we pop the number of objects specified by the argument count, then the function itself. Then, we determine if it's a built-in or user-defined function (or an error).

```
func (vm *VM) executeFunctionCall(fr *frame, argCount int) (
    fnReturn object.Object, err error) {

    args := vm.popMultiple(argCount)
    fn := vm.pop()

    switch fn := fn.(type) {
    case *object.CompiledCode:
        fnReturn, _, err = vm.runCompiledCode(fn, fr, args, nil)
    case *object.BuiltIn:
        fnReturn, err = vm.callBuiltIn(fn, fr, args)
    default:
        return nil, fmt.Errorf(
            "Call operation on non-function (%s)",
            object.TypeDescription(fn.Type()))
    }

    return fnReturn, err
}
```

Here we see `fnReturn` again. This is where it is caught. If there is no error, we push the `fnReturn` value onto the stack in the instruction loop.

In calling `vm.runCompiledCode( )`, we use an underscore in the list of values to receive from it, because we're ignoring a return value for a jump relay, as a function would not use it directly.

function opcodes

We'll use our factorial function as an example for opcodes. Let's go to the REPL.

```
>> val .factorial = f if(.x < 2: 1; .x x self(.x - 1))
ByteCode Instructions
0000 Constant 3
0003 SetGlobal 4
0006 Pop

ByteCode Constants
1: Number 2
2: Number 1
3: Function factorial (...); ParameterCount: 1; LocalBindingsCount: 1
Instructions
0000 GetLocal 0
0002 Constant 1
0005 LessThan 0 0
0009 JumpIfNotTruthy 8
0014 Constant 2
0017 Jump 12
0022 GetLocal 0
0024 GetSelf
0025 GetLocal 0
0027 Constant 2
0030 Subtract
0031 Call 1
0033 Multiply
0034 ReturnValue
```

```
langur escaped result: function .factorial
```

We start with `0000 Constant 3`, our factorial function. Then, `0003 SetGlobal 4` sets an immutable variable called `.factorial` to this function.

Moving to the function instructions, `0000 GetLocal 0` is the parameter `.x`. Parameters are always at the beginning of a function frame's locals slice. *If* expressions are described in the "if / given expressions" chapter. There are a couple of notable things in these opcodes. `0024 GetSelf` is a self-reference used for recursive functions. In langur, we can use the `self` token, or if assigned directly to a variable, we can use the function name within the function.

This code does not execute the function. At the end the function's instructions, an OpReturnValue (`0034 ReturnValue` above) would cause the value at the top of the stack to be used as the function's return value (passed as `fnReturn` in Go as a function frame exits). If we take a quick look at this opcode in the VM instruction loop again, we see the following.

```
case opcode.OpReturnValue:
    fnReturn = vm.pop()
    return
```

This exits the immediate frame, but it might be a frame within a function frame and not the function itself. That is why, at the end of the instruction loop, after all the case statement tests, we have the following.

```
if fnReturn != nil {
    return
}
```

So, this will back out of all frames until it reaches the `executeFunctionCall()` method we just looked at.

Let us execute the function we defined and see the opcodes to do so.

```
>> .factorial(7)
ByteCode Instructions
0000 GetGlobal 4
0003 Constant 4
0006 Call 1
0008 Pop

ByteCode Constants
...
3: Function factorial (...); ParameterCount: 1; LocalBindingsCount: 1
...
4: Number 7

langur escaped result: 5040
```

`0000 GetGlobal` `4` first retrieves the function we defined earlier (pushes to the top of the stack), then `0003 Constant` `4` pushes a number `7`. Then, `0006 Call` `1` instructs the VM to execute a function call with 1 argument. The VM pulls the argument off the stack first, then the function, then executes the function, and pushes the result.

closures

Langur began as a sort-of functional style language. It retains the "purity" of functions, in that they cannot change values from outside their boundaries.[9] They can, however, access those values as closures.

A "free" variable is any variable accessed from outside a closure. If any of these are present, a function is a "closure," as it is said to "close over" a value. In all the things I've read, this is not explained clearly, so let me add another poor attempt.

---

9   Langur functions are not pure in regards to "side effects." That is, they may call built-ins like `writeln()`.

In langur, a closure will receive the values of its free variables from the VM (at run-time; not known at compile-time), at the point of the closure's definition in the code. It will then place these values onto the CompiledCode object's Free objects slice.[10]

Using the REPL, we can see this if we declare a mutable value, use it within a function definition, try the function, change the mutable value, and try the function again. We see that the function's return value does not change. In the following, it "closed over" the value of .x at the point of the function's definition, so when .x is redefined, it does not affect the function definition or change its return value. Thus, it is a "free" variable within the function.

```
>> var .x = 7
langur escaped result: 7

>> val .add = f(.i) .i + .x
langur escaped result: function .add

>> .add(123)
langur escaped result: 130

>> .x = 21
langur escaped result: 21

>> .add(123)
langur escaped result: 130
```

We see the same return value, even though we changed .x after defining .add, which definition included .x. The definition of .add received the value of .x at a single point of execution, and not a reference to it.

---

10 Actually, as designed at this time, it copies the CompiledCode object first. See the definition of pushClosure() and explanation at "pushing closures in the VM."

pushing closures in the VM

Regular functions are pushed onto the stack with a simple OpConstant. But how are closures pushed onto the stack? In the instruction loop, we see the following case.

```
case opcode.OpClosure:
    constIndex := int(opcode.ReadUInt16(ins[ip+1:]))
    freeCount := int(ins[ip+3])
    ip += 3
    err = vm.pushClosure(fr, constIndex, freeCount)
```

Before this OpClosure is reached, the VM has executed instructions that put all the free variables' values onto the top of the stack. This makes it possible for vm.pushClosure() to put these values into the Free objects slice on a CompiledCode object.

```
func (vm *VM) pushClosure(fr *frame, constIndex, freeCount int) error {
    constant := vm.constants[constIndex]
    compiledFn, ok := constant.(*object.CompiledCode)
    if !ok {
        bug("pushClosure", fmt.Sprintf("Not a function: %T", constant))
        return fmt.Errorf("Not a function: %T", constant)
    }

    compiledFn = compiledFn.Copy().(*object.CompiledCode)

    compiledFn.Free = vm.popMultiple(freeCount)
    return vm.push(compiledFn)
}
```

You may notice that we copy the CompiledCode object before setting the Free objects slice. This ensures that if there is a single compiled closure with multiple definitions and assignments, that they don't clobber each other's free objects. I have tested this possibility, and this was a necessary addition for langur. There's no telling how someone may code.

closure opcodes

Using a simple addition function with one value accessed from outside of it is sufficient to see closure opcodes.

```
>> val .add = f(.i) .i + .x
ByteCode Instructions
0000 GetGlobal 4
0003 Closure 2 1
0007 SetGlobal 5
0010 Pop

ByteCode Constants
1: Number 7
2: Function add (...); ParameterCount: 1; LocalBindingsCount: 1
Instructions
0000 GetLocal 0
0002 GetFree 0
0004 Add
0005 ReturnValue

langur escaped result: function .add
```

In these instructions, before defining our closure, we gather our "free" variable values. `0000 GetGlobal 4` retrieves the value of `.x`. Then, `0003 Closure 2 1` tells the VM to use constant 2 and 1 free variable value, which we just pushed onto the stack. Then, with `0007 SetGlobal 5`, we set a new immutable called `.add`.

Again, this does not execute the function call, but only defines the function, setting the values of its free variables at the same time. In the function closure instructions, you'll notice `0002 GetFree 0` (free value saved from variable `.x`), which retrieves a value from the frame's `Free` objects slice at index 0, pushing it onto the stack. Since the value now sits inside the function definition, "closed over," we can change the value of `.x` outside the function, and it does not affect the closure function's results.

compiling user-defined functions

To compile user-defined functions, the first thing we do is push variable scope.

```
func (c *Compiler) compileFunctionNode(node *ast.FunctionNode) (
    ins opcode.Instructions, err error) {

    c.pushVariableScope(true)
    c.functionLevel++

    defer func() {
        c.popVariableScope()
        c.functionLevel--
    }()
```

What is the counter `c.functionLevel` for? We check its value when compiling a `return` statement to see if it was used outside of a function, which is illegal in langur.

The `defer` will execute `c.popVariableScope()` whenever we exit the method `compileFunctionNode()`, without having to keep track of it going forward.[11]

We pass the Boolean `true` to `c.pushVariableScope()` to indicate that this scope is a function so that a flag will be set on the new symbol table. This enables the compiler package symbol tables to ensure that functions do not set any values outside of their boundaries, since non-function scopes are allowed to change values outside their boundaries, but functions are not.

```
if node.Name != "" {
    c.symbolTable.defineSelf(node.Name)
}
```

---

11 Go creates a stack of deferred calls that are executed in the opposite order of their definition when a function exits. This can be very useful, as you can add a `defer` to close a resource as soon as you open it, or use it as shown here. Evaluation of arguments to a deferred call are not deferred.

We check if the function is assigned to a variable (if `node.Name` was set by the parser), in part so we can use the name within the function body to refer to itself. (Or, we could use a `self` token in langur whether the function has a name or not.)

Then, we add all the function parameters to our symbol table.

```go
for i, p := range node.Parameters {
    v, ok := p.(*ast.VariableNode)
    if !ok {
        return nil, makeErr(node,
            fmt.Sprintf("Parameter %d not a variable", i+1))
    }
    _, err = c.symbolTable.defineUserVariable(v.Name, true)
    if err != nil {
        err = makeErr(node, fmt.Sprintf(
            "Parameter %d definition error: %s", i+1, err.Error()))
    }
}
```

Once we have the parameters defined, we can compile the function body, and add an OpReturnValue if necessary (if not ending with a "definite jump" already). We must compile the body after defining parameters, as we expect to use them therein. We're still in the same variable scope we pushed at the beginning.

```go
body, err = c.compileNode(node.Body, false)
if err != nil {
    return
}

if len(body) == 0 {
    // no body; return no value
    body = append(c.noValueIns, opcode.Make(opcode.OpReturnValue)...)

} else if !ast.EndsWithDefiniteJump(node.Body.(*ast.BlockNode).Statements) {
    // append return if doesn't already end with return
    body = append(body, opcode.Make(opcode.OpReturnValue)...)
}
```

Next, we gather "free" symbols and the locals count from the symbol table. The locals count includes both the parameters and any first-level declarations within the function body (not in another scope within the function).

```
freeSymbols := c.symbolTable.FreeSymbols
localsCount := c.symbolTable.definitionCount
```

We now have the information to create a CompileCode object for the function. We don't have to use a variable as follows (compiledFn), but it makes it clean and clear.

```
compiledFn := &object.CompiledCode{
    Name:               node.Name,
    IsFunction:         true,
    Instructions:       body,
    LocalBindingsCount: localsCount,
    ParameterCount:     len(node.Parameters),
}
fnIndex := c.addConstant(compiledFn)
```

We saved the "body" instructions to a variable, which we saved to the `Instructions` field of a new CompiledCode object, which we saved to the constants slice, and we've saved an index number to refer to it (`fnIndex`). At this point, we begin building opcode instructions that will put a function onto the stack.

If we had any free symbols, we create opcodes to push them onto the stack prior to an OpClosure instruction. Otherwise, we only generate an OpConstant. Then, having used Go named return value `ins`, we return from `compileFunctionNode()`.

```
if len(freeSymbols) > 0 {
    // a closure
    ins = nil
    for _, sym := range freeSymbols {
        val, err := c.makeOpGetInstructions(node, sym, 0)
        if err != nil {
            return nil, err
        }
        ins = append(ins, val...)
    }
    ins = append(ins, opcode.Make(
        opcode.OpClosure, fnIndex, len(freeSymbols))...)

} else {
    // not a closure
    ins = opcode.Make(opcode.OpConstant, fnIndex)
}

return
}
```

That's it. Our user-defined functions are compiled and ready for use.

compiling function calls

To compile a function call, first we check for an argument / parameter count mismatch. It's not always possible to do this in langur at compile-time, so we might not get a compile error, but still have an error in the VM, but if it is a built-in function call, we know that we know the parameter limits.

```
func (c *Compiler) compileCallNode(node *ast.CallNode) (
    ins opcode.Instructions, err error) {

    err = c.checkArgumentParameterCount(node)
    if err != nil {
        return
    }
```

Then, we compile the function node itself, which may be a function literal, a built-in, or a variable retrieval of a built-in or user-defined function.

```go
ins, err = c.compileNode(node.Function, true)
if err != nil {
    return
}
```

Then the arguments.

```go
var bslc []byte
for _, arg := range node.Args {
    bslc, err = c.compileNode(arg, true)
    if err != nil {
        break
    }
    ins = append(ins, bslc...)
}
```

Now, having compiled instructions for each argument, using the argument count, we build one more instruction and tack it onto the end.

```go
    ins = append(ins, opcode.Make(opcode.OpCall, len(node.Args))...)
    return
}
```

This is the same for user-defined function calls or built-in function calls. When you call c.compileNode(node.Function, true), the compiler will handle whatever type of node it is and build the necessary opcode instructions. We've already looked at how to compile user-defined functions. Next, we'll look at how to deal with built-in functions.

12
built-in functions

Langur includes several useful built-in functions. Some of my favorites are `map()` and `fold()`, as these can do several things you would do with a loop, without having to write a loop. Functional style functions can shorten source code, as well.

The built-in functions (or just "built-ins") are located in the builtins package. There, we have a slice of `*object.BuiltIn`. To be available to langur source code, a function must have an entry in this slice. Internal built-ins are also listed so they can be used from the AST, but not from source code. The names of internal built-ins start with an underscore.

```
var BuiltIns = []*object.BuiltIn{
    // internal built-ins
    &object.BuiltIn{
        Name: "_limit", Fn: bi__limit,
        ParamMin: 1, ParamMax: 1},

    &object.BuiltIn{
        Name: "_values", Fn: bi__values,
        ParamMin: 1, ParamMax: 1},
```

```
// external built-ins
&object.BuiltIn{
    Name: "abs", Fn: bi_abs,
    Description: "returns the absolute value of a number",
    ParamMin:    1, ParamMax: 1},

&object.BuiltIn{
    Name: "all", Fn: bi_all,
    Description: "all(validation, array); returns Boolean ...",
    ParamMin:    2, ParamMax: 2},

    ...
```

Every built-in has the same signature (except for the name, of course). Looking at object/functions.go, we see the following type declarations.

```
type BuiltInFunction func(cc *CallChannels, args ...Object) Object

type BuiltIn struct {
    Fn          BuiltInFunction
    Name        string
    Description string
    ParamMin    int
    ParamMax    int
}
```

And, in builtins/map.go, we see the following for map(), matching the signature for object.BuiltInFunction.

```
func bi_map(cc *object.CallChannels, args ...object.Object) object.Object {
    ...
}
```

So, each built-in receives a pointer to a CallChannels struct (located in the object package) and a slice of argument objects, and returns an object (actually a pointer to an object, with object.Object being a Go interface).

I wanted built-ins to be able to execute user-defined functions (to make `map()`, etc. possible), and this requires that they are able to use the VM. There may be a better way, but having kept built-ins separate from the VM, they have to be able to communicate with each other. As you'll see shortly, we're using Go channels for communication, and not for concurrency. We can't have both packages import each other. Go would fail to compile this and smack us with a "circular dependency" error.

Let us take a look inside object/functions.go to see what these structures look like.

```
type ExternalReceiveResult struct {
    Result Object
    Error  error
}

type ExternalCallCompiledFunction struct {
    Fn            *CompiledCode
    Args          []Object
    ReceiveResult chan *ExternalReceiveResult
}

type CallChannels struct {
    CallCompiledChan  chan *ExternalCallCompiledFunction
    SaveReceiveResult chan *ExternalReceiveResult
    Modes             *modes.VmModes
}
```

So, a call channel passes along the information a built-in needs to send a function to the VM. It also passes along VM modes, for things like case insensitive mode.

It does not pass along `SaveReceiveResult`. This is used within the builtins package itself to build a channel once and save it for more sequential (non-concurrent) calls to the VM. Does it save time to build it only once? The answer is ... I can't tell.

built-ins in the VM

As we saw in the chapter on "user-defined functions," a function call is made in the instruction loop via OpCall, for built-ins and user-defined functions.

```
case opcode.OpCall:
    argCount := int(ins[ip+1])
    ip += 1

    result, err = vm.executeFunctionCall(fr, argCount)
    if err == nil {
        err = vm.push(result)
    }
```

If vm.executeFunctionCall() finds a built-in function instead of a user-defined function, it calls vm.callBuiltIn(). This function begins by building it's needed channels.

```
func (vm *VM) callBuiltIn(
    bi *object.BuiltIn, fr *frame, args []object.Object) (
    result object.Object, err error) {

    finished := make(chan bool)
    compiledChan := make(chan *object.ExternalCallCompiledFunction)
```

We can't just build these channels once and reuse them, as we can't be sure about nesting of calls. A built-in might call a user-defined function that calls a built-in. If we reused these channels, we'd be in trouble, so we build new ones for each call.

Then, we execute a goroutine, including a defer to catch any panics and to send a finished signal when done. Note that the Go operator <- is used to send and receive data over channels and will block as necessary, waiting either to send or receive.

```
go func() {
    defer func() {
        // to catch panic on this goroutine
        if p := recover(); p != nil {
            err = object.NewErrorFromAnything(p, "panic:"+bi.Name)
```

```
        }

        // send finished signal, whether there was a panic or not
        finished <- true
    }()

    result, err = builtins.Call(bi, compiledChan, vm.modes, args)
}()
```

Why use a goroutine? We don't know if the built-in we call is going to ask to run a user-defined function, or maybe several.

We use a select statement after launching the goroutine to receive all such requests. The *for* loop enables us to respond to multiple requests from a built-in (sequentially), then break when the finished signal is received from the deferred function in the goroutine above. The finished signal will not be sent until `builtins.Call()` has returned, with or without a panic, and this will not happen in the middle of a response because the builtin is blocked awaiting the response from the VM, and we will look at this shortly.

```
fini: // label to directly break from for loop from inside select
    for {
        select {
        case ecc := <-compiledChan:
            // received request from built-in to call compiled function
            eccResult, _, eccErr := vm.runCompiledCode(
                ecc.Fn, fr, ecc.Args, nil)

            // return result of compiled function call to the built-in
            ecc.ReceiveResult <- &object.ExternalReceiveResult{
                Result: eccResult, Error: eccErr}

        case <-finished:
            // finished signal from goroutine that called the built-in
            break fini
        }
    }
```

And last of all, we check if the result we received was `nil` and set it to `object.NO_DATA` if so. Then, returning from the function, the named return values of `result` and `err` are automatically returned from `callBuiltIn()`.

```
    if result == nil {
        result = object.NO_DATA
    }
    return
}
```

The instruction loop includes code to push the result of a function call to the stack. It may have returned a langur exception as a Go error. We discuss langur exceptions in the "exceptions" chapter, but it should suffice for now to know that langur error objects also match the Go Error interface and are passed along as errors.

That's for a call to a built-in. But how is a built-in put onto the stack in the first place? In the instruction loop, we have a `case` for an OpGetBuiltIn, which retrieves an `*object.BuiltIn` directly from the `builtins.BuiltIns` slice, using the index that was passed.

```
case opcode.OpGetBuiltIn:
    biIndex := opcode.ReadUInt16(ins[ip+1:])
    ip += 2
    err = vm.push(builtins.BuiltIns[biIndex])
```

calls to built-ins in the builtins package

So, what happens in the builtins package? In a goroutine we just looked at, the VM executes `builtins.Call()`. We see this function in the source file builtins/call.go.

```
func Call(
    fn *object.BuiltIn,
    compiledChan chan *object.ExternalCallCompiledFunction,
    modes *modes.VmModes,
    args []object.Object) (

    object.Object, error) {
```

```
    // not building a receive result channel unless we need it ...
    // ... (actually make a call to the VM from a built-in)
    cc := &object.CallChannels{CallCompiledChan: compiledChan, Modes: modes}

    // some functions give trouble if we don't copy the arguments slice
    args = object.CopyRefSlice(args)

    return call(fn, cc, args...)
}
```

Called from the VM, this puts together a CallChannels object for the built-in to use, with VM modes piggybacking. We copy the arguments slice, because otherwise we run into trouble when the references change from "under our feet," so to speak. The "exportable" Call() function calls the local call() function,[12] which is located in the same source file. This local call() function is also what the built-ins use to call other functions that were passed to them.

Let us look at the call() function in two parts. First, we see how it deals with a call to a built-in function. This is accomplished with "result := fn.Fn(cc, args...)". This call to a built-in could have originated in the VM or from another built-in function.

```
func call(fn object.Object,
    cc *object.CallChannels,
    args ...object.Object) (

    object.Object, error) {

    switch fn := fn.(type) {
    case *object.BuiltIn:
        if BuiltInArgCountMismatch(fn, len(args)) {
            return nil, object.NewError(object.ERR_ARGUMENTS, fn.Name,
                "Argument/Parameter Count Mismatch")
        }
```

----

12 In Go, use a capital letter to begin the name of anything you define to be "exportable" from a package (that is, accessible from outside the package), and a lowercase letter for anything that isn't.

```
    result := fn.Fn(cc, args...)
    if result.Type() == object.ERROR_OBJ {
        return nil, result.(*object.Error)
    } else {
        return result, nil
    }
```

In the second half of this function, we see how it deals with a call to a user-defined function. This means that a built-in has made a call to `call()` with a user-defined function. This is where we use the channels to communicate with the VM. We already received a channel to send communication to the VM. Now, we build a channel to receive a result from the VM, if not already done. Then, we include that channel in the information we pass to the VM (`*object.ExternalCallCompiledFunction`), so the VM can use it to return the result. The code "`result := <-cc.SaveReceiveResult`" will block until a communication is received from the channel. Note that since we wrote the code for both sides of the channel, we know there will only be one result sent.[13] Getting back to the second half of `call()`...

```
    case *object.CompiledCode:
        // since a sequential (non-concurrent) call, ...
        // ... make recieve result channel once and save for reuse
        if cc.SaveReceiveResult == nil {
            cc.SaveReceiveResult = make(chan *object.ExternalReceiveResult)
        }

        cc.CallCompiledChan <- &object.ExternalCallCompiledFunction{
            Fn: fn, Args: args,
            ReceiveResult: cc.SaveReceiveResult,
        }
        result := <-cc.SaveReceiveResult

        return result.Result, result.Error
    }
```

---

13 Channels can be used to send many values, and seem like a great way to deal with communication in a concurrent model, but I digress.

```
      return nil, fmt.Errorf("Not a callable object (%T)", fn)
}
```

Could we not have built the receive result channel in the VM and just passed it along? Yes, and I originally set it up that way. But, I like it better this way, because it seems more flexible. Each side declares it's own channels to receive information and passes that along to the other half.

built-in call opcodes

To call a built-in, the opcodes essentially look the same as for a user-defined function call, except that we have an OpGetBuiltIn to retrieve the desired function instead of OpConstant or OpClosure or a variable set to a function (retrieved with OpGetGlobal, OpGetLocal, etc.).

Let us use the built-in `len()` function in the REPL. In this example, it happens to be indexed at 44, but this could change.

```
>> len [7, 21, 14]
ByteCode Instructions
0000 GetBuiltIn 44
0003 Constant 1
0006 Constant 2
0009 Constant 3
0012 Array 3
0015 Call 1
0017 Pop

ByteCode Constants
1: Number 7
2: Number 21
3: Number 14

langur escaped result: 3
```

We first see `0000 GetBuiltIn 44`, then its one argument, which is prepared by the next 4 opcodes. Then, `0015 Call 1` says to make a function call with one argument. At the point of the OpCall, the top of the stack is an array object containing 3 elements, and the next thing down is the built-in function we retrieved at the beginning. Receiving OpCall, the VM will pop the arguments and the function, and push the result.

compiling built-in calls / references

Compiling a call to a built-in is the same as compiling a call to a user-defined function. See that in the chapter on "user-defined functions." Before the call, there would be an opcode to put the built-in onto the stack.

Compiling a reference to a built-in, to put it onto the stack, is simple....

```go
func (c *Compiler) compileBuiltInNode(node *ast.BuiltInNode) (
    ins opcode.Instructions, err error) {

    idx, ok := builtins.GetBuiltInIndex(node.Name)
    if !ok {
        err = makeErr(node,
            fmt.Sprintf("Unknown token used %s", node.Name))

        return
    }

    ins = opcode.Make(opcode.OpGetBuiltIn, idx)
    return
}
```

So, we get the index for a specific built-in function and generate an opcode to retrieve it. Easy peasy.

13

for loops

For loops are a generally universal concept in programming. A typical *for* loop has 3 sections listed before the body of the loop, separated by 2 semicolons, with the body enclosed in curly braces.

You could skip to "example 3 part for loop in langur" if this bores you.

typical for loop layout

for *initialization*; *test*; *increment* { *body* }

A *for* loop will execute the *body* section repeatedly until the *test* is negative or an explicit means of breaking from the loop is used (such as a *break* statement). If the *test* is negative at the start, the loop will not run at all. Between each iteration, the *increment* will be executed.

example 3 part for loop in Go

```
for i := 0; i < len(somearray); i++ {
    fmt.Fprintf("%d\n", somearray[i])
}
```

In the example above, the variable i will give you index values to use with the `somearray` variable in the *body* of the loop. In this simple example, we just write each value to the console (with `somearray` as an array of integers).

We initialize a new variable i to 0. In Go, the := operator not only assigns, but is a declaration with implicit typing.

In the *increment* section, the ++ operator adds one to the current value of the variable i. This will be done each time after the *body* section is executed.

Many languages, including Go, use 0-based indexing as this was seen as being more efficient. Let's say we have an array of length 7 (has 7 elements). These elements would be indexed from 0 to 6. So, the *test* code "i < `len`(`somearray`)" would mean that when i gets to be 7, it's out of range (cannot be used to index `somearray`), so it's time to exit the loop.

example 3 part for loop in langur

Langur uses 1-based indexing as it is more friendly to human beings. Therefore, though the example below does the same as the one above, it initializes the loop variable to 1 and uses the less-than-or-equal operator (<=) rather than the less-than operator (<) used in the Go language example. Also, as of writing, langur had no ++ operator, so we use a combination += operator to increment variable .i.

```
for .i = 1; .i <= len(.somearray); .i += 1 {
    writeln .somearray[.i]
}
```

In langur, assignment in the *initialization* section of a *for* loop is automatically taken as declaration.

The entire loop will have scope, so that loop variables are confined to it.

for loop expression opcodes

We'll start with opcodes. Then, we'll talk about how to compile them. For loops in langur have 4 sections, which correlate directly to the 3 part *for* loop.

The 4 sections are (in order):

1. initialization
2. test
       conditional jump out
3. body
4. increment
       jump back to test

The initialization is done only once. Every execution of the body section is preceded by a test. If the test fails, we jump out of the loop (over all remaining opcodes in the loop) and we're done. If it succeeds, we execute the body section, then the increment section. With the increment done, we jump back to the beginning of the test section's opcodes. There are no jumps between the initialization and test sections, so one opcode follows another without any clear delineation. Ditto the body and increment sections. (I will point these out as we go.)

So, what kind of opcodes do we get from a simple loop? First, let's initialize an array in the REPL. I'll leave out these opcodes from here (explained elsewhere).

```
>> val .arr = series 1..7
```

Now, using the REPL, I get the following.

```
>> for .i = 1; .i <= len(.arr); .i += 1 { writeln .arr[.i] }
ByteCode Instructions
0000 Execute 3
0003 Pop
```

```
ByteCode Constants
1: Number 1
2: Number 7
3: Code (...); LocalBindingsCount: 1
Instructions
0000 Null
0001 Constant 1
0004 SetLocal 0
0006 Pop
0007 GetLocal 0
0009 GetBuiltIn 47
0012 GetGlobal 4
0015 Call 1
0017 LessThanOrEqual 0 0
0021 JumpIfNotTruthy 26
0026 GetBuiltIn 102
0029 GetGlobal 4
0032 GetLocal 0
0034 Index
0035 Call 1
0037 Pop
0038 GetLocal 0
0040 Constant 1
0043 Add
0044 SetLocal 0
0046 Pop
0047 JumpBack 40
```

Let's go over this real quickly.

First, langur uses frames for variable scope (among other things). That's why we start with OpExecute, which is a scoped *for* loop in this case. This is followed with OpPop to remove the value created by the loop.

Looking at the "ByteCode Constants," there are four of them. Constant 0 is the langur revision number (the system variable _rev), which we can ignore. The number 7 (constant 2) is lingering in the REPL from an earlier use (when we initialized the array we're using). The number 1 (constant 1) is also lingering, but otherwise would come from the initialization and the increment sections, which both contain a 1.

Constant 3 (the fourth one) is the *for* loop itself. It starts with OpNull to ensure something is on the stack when the loop is exited. This is the default value a langur *for* loop generates. You could use break with a specified value and the loop will evaluate to that instead. (We get to break and next at the end of this chapter.) I'm most languages, I believe it's typical that *for* loops are statements, not expressions, and don't produce values.

Ignoring the null on the stack until we get to the end...

OpConstant is the next opcode. This makes reference to constant 1, which in this case just happens to be the number 1.

Next, we initialize the local value of .i. We have SetLocal 0. This sets local scope frame value 0 (.i) to the constant that we just put on the stack (1). Next, we need an OpPop to take the value off the stack. That's the end of our simple initialization section.

0007 OpGetLocal 0 begins the test section. This retrieves local scope value 0.

So, between the initialization and test, why do we use OpPop to drop and then OpGetLocal to get the same value? The world is imperfect. The test section likely needs to be repeated, whereas initialization happens once.

Then, we have GetBuiltIn 47. This retrieves a reference to the built-in len() function, indexed among the built-ins at 47. (The value could be different than this.) Then, we have 0012 GetGlobal 4, which is the variable .arr which I set earlier. Now, we have 3 things we've put on the stack in a specific order (ignoring the null we first put on the stack, which would make 4 things).

0015 Call 1 tells the VM to execute the function, sending it the arguments, and if there isn't an exception, the VM will receive a value from the function. (All functions in langur return something, even if it's `null`.) The VM will push the return value onto the stack. This call popped the built-in and the global we just pushed.

Now, we have two things we've put on the stack, as we have not removed the value set from constant 1, representing the number `1` in this case. The second thing (the top of the stack) is the return value from the function, giving the length of the array.

With two values to consider on the stack, we now have `0017 LessThanOrEqual 0 0`. We'll ignore the two operands `0  0` for now. (One is a set of enumeration flags to indicate whether it is a database operator and such, and the other a number representing how far to jump for a short-circuiting operator.) Seeing OpLessThanOrEqual and no short-circuiting, the VM will pop two values off the stack and compare them with the operator and push the result. Now, we have one Boolean value at the top of the stack.

Next comes `0021 JumpIfNotTruthy 26`. This would jump out of the *for* loop (past `0047 JumpBack 40`), as a failed test indicates that we're done. The Boolean value will be popped off the stack before we jump or continue.

Continuing, the body section begins with `0026 GetBuiltIn 102`, which retrieves the `writeln()` function in this case. Then, we retrieve the `.arr` variable with `GetGlobal 4`, then the variable `.i` with `GetLocal 0`. An OpIndex pops two values off the stack (from `.arr` and `.i`), does the index operation, and pushes the result. `0035 Call 1` calls the `writeln()` function we pushed earlier with the one argument (the index result) and pops both of these, pushing the result of the function call. We have OpPop at byte `0037` to clean up the stack. This is the end of the body section.

The increment section begins by retrieving `.i` with `0038 GetLocal 0` and the number `1` with `0040 Constant 1`. It adds these with `0043 Add` (popping both). Then, `0044 SetLocal 0` sets `.i` to the stack result and `0046 Pop` cleans up. This would be the end of the increment section, but for one thing. The VM would not know to go back to the test if we didn't tell it to. So, `0047 JumpBack 40` tells the VM to go back 40 bytes in the instruction set.

What happens if the test result is "not truthy" and we jump past the OpJumpBack? We're out of instructions in the *for* loop scope frame. What should the VM do now? It takes the value at the top of the stack. Remember that OpNull we used earlier? That's all that's on the stack. As we showed earlier, as we exit a frame, a deferred function resets the stack, leaving just the last value at the top (null in this case).

Using break with an expression value, we could cause a *for* loop to evaluate with something other than null. It will push the value to the top of the stack right before the *break* happens. It doesn't matter that the null is also on the stack, as only the top value will be preserved when the frame of the *for* loop is exited. We will look at the compileBreak() method shortly, and you'll see that it begins with instructions that will push a value. (The parser has insured that if anything is attached to a break statement, it is an expression producing a value.)

Now, we've exited back to the global frame and have a value on the stack, but we're done. What now? Clean up, of course. It uses OpPop and pops this value off the stack.

Reviewing the 4 sections, we have the following codes. I've added comments preceded with hash marks.

```
# start of initialization
0001 Constant 1
...
# start of test
0007 GetLocal 0
...
# end of test
0021 JumpIfNotTruthy 26
# start of body
0026 GetBuiltIn 102
...
# start of increment
0038 GetLocal 0
...
```

```
# jump back to test
0047 JumpBack 40
```

compiling for loop expressions

Besides the 3 part *for* loop, langur has other types of *for* loops, but the compiler only builds one format. The parser and ast packages convert the other types of langur loops as necessary into 3 part *for* loops before the compiler sees them. Because of this and the universality of the 3 part loop, we'll discuss only that here.

How do we compile these things and figure out how far to jump? That's a good question. I'm glad you asked.

In compiler/flow.go, we find the `compileFor()` method, accepting a pointer to a `ForNode` and returning instructions and an `error` (`nil` for no error).

First, you'll notice a section of code that deals with scope. We usually need scope on a *for* loop, so we just assume that we will.

```go
func (c *Compiler) compileFor(node *ast.ForNode) (
    ins opcode.Instructions, err error) {

    var init, test, body, increment []byte

    c.pushVariableScope(false)
    defer func() {
        ins = c.wrapInstructionsWithExecute(ins)
        c.popVariableScope()
    }()
```

The `pushVariableScope()` method gives a new symbol table to use (discussed earlier). Then, using `defer` causes code to be run as we exit the function, and not before.

When we call the `wrapInstructionsWithExecute()` method, it creates a new constant containing the "wrapped" instructions, then returns an OpExecute instruction using this constant as the index. This method also must know how many variables are in scope, so we simply use it before we pop the scope. When popped, we revert to the previous symbol table (a link to which had been saved in the new symbol table when we pushed variable scope in the compiler). Remember, the symbol table is for the compiler only. The VM sees none of it.

First, we set up instructions in separate byte slices, to help us determine how to set jumps. Note the byte slices declared at the beginning of the function.

```
var init, test, body, increment []byte
```

We initialize the `init` slice by adding the `null` value. This causes *for* loops, being expressions, to produce `null` by default. Then, we go through the initializations and compile those first. If we tried to compile the other sections first, the loop variables would not be in our symbol table, and the compiler would balk instead of doing useful things. And who needs that?

```
// making sure something is on the stack
init = c.noValueIns

for _, each := range node.Init {
    var i []byte
    i, err = c.compileNode(each, true)
    if err != nil {
        return
    }
    init = append(init, i...)
}
```

The `*ast.ForNode` field `Init` (seen as `node.Init` above) is a slice of initialization instructions, each of which directly correlates to a part of a comma-delimited list in the *for* loop initialization section. Again, we use `true` in `compileNode()` to ensure it pops at the end. In our example, the initialization created the following opcodes.

```
0001 Constant 1
0004 SetLocal 0
0006 Pop
```

We have only one initialization here, so it's relatively simple. This is just an assignment. We get a constant, set the local variable, and pop the constant off the stack. Why is it OpSetLocal? Because the *for* loop is in a scope of its own and this refers directly to a variable within the frame and scope, in this case, of the *for* loop.

Back to the compiler... Next, we compile the test, the body, and the increments (a comma-delimited list in langur source code), without knowing how far to set jumps for.

```
if node.Test != nil {
    test, err = c.compileNode(node.Test, true)
    if err != nil {
        return
    }
}

body, err = c.compileNode(node.Body, true)
if err != nil {
    return
}

for _, each := range node.Increment {
    var i []byte
    i, err = c.compileNode(each, true)
    if err != nil {
        return
    }
    increment = append(increment, i...)
}
```

Having compiled each section independently, we know how far each jump needs to be, so we append those to the instructions for the test and increment sections. Below, you see `opcode.OP_JUMP_LEN` added to the jump distance from the test because the jump is not yet added to the increment (next line).

```
if len(test) > 0 {
    test = append(test, opcode.Make(opcode.OpJumpIfNotTruthy,
        len(body)+len(increment)+opcode.OP_JUMP_LEN)...)
}
increment = append(increment, opcode.Make(opcode.OpJumpBack,
    len(test)+len(body)+len(increment))...)
```

We put all the sections together, and as we exit, the deferred function is called to finish the scope business discussed earlier. But, we skipped something....

break and next

I haven't discussed something vital to *for* loops yet. We also have `break` and `next` statements. A `break` lets you break directly out of a loop. Do not increment, do not test, do not pass Go. A `next` (*continue* in some languages) jumps out of the current position in the body to the increment section. This will increment and test again, thus trying the next iteration.

Did I mention that langur uses relative jumps? This being the case, we have to know how far to jump, not really "where" to jump to in the instruction set. So, how do we set the jumps for `break` and `next`? We use placeholders first. How do we know a placeholder is going to be reset by the right *for* loop when they are nested? Recursion. An inner loop compilation will finish resetting jumps before returning it's instructions to an outer loop compilation. Then, the outer loop compilation gets to reset jumps, but it doesn't see the placeholders from the inner loop, because they're already gone.

Compiling placeholders looks something like the following. These are functions called by `compileNode()` when it encounters a `BreakNode` or `NextNode`, as it might in compiling the *for* loop body.

```
func (c *Compiler) compileBreak(node *ast.BreakNode) (
    ins opcode.Instructions, err error) {

    c.breakStmtCount++

    if node.Value != nil {
        // break with value
        ins, err = c.compileNode(node.Value, false)
    }

    ins = append(ins, opcode.Make(opcode.OpJumpPlaceHolder,
        opcode.OC_PlaceHolder_Break)...)

    return
}

func (c *Compiler) compileNext(node *ast.NextNode) (
    ins opcode.Instructions, err error) {

    c.nextStmtCount++
    ins = opcode.Make(opcode.OpJumpPlaceHolder, opcode.OC_PlaceHolder_Next)
    return
}
```

Since we're setting placeholders, we use `c.breakStmtCount++` and `c.nextStmtCount++` to ensure all of them are accounted for when the compiler is done. We decrement these counts as we replace placeholders. If someone tries to use `break` or `next` outside of a *for* loop, for example, this would be an error. The compiler will check the counts when it is done and generate an error if they are not 0. I'd rather have the compiler fail on this than have the VM panic for an unrecognized opcode (such as OpJumpPlaceholder). It's good to avoid panics.

Having compiled *for* loop instructions using placeholders for `break` and `next` (if present), after compiling the body, we call a method called `fixJumps()` twice, passing it the maximum length we want to jump and the frame level 0.

```
body = c.fixJumps(body, false, opcode.OC_PlaceHolder_Next,
    &c.nextStmtCount, len(body), 0, 0)

body = c.fixJumps(body, false, opcode.OC_PlaceHolder_Break,
    &c.breakStmtCount, len(body)+len(increment)+opcode.OP_JUMP_LEN, 0, 0)
```

Then, we add our other jumps (as we looked at earlier), put the instructions together and return from the compileFor() method.

```
    if len(test) > 0 {
        test = append(test, opcode.Make(opcode.OpJumpIfNotTruthy,
            len(body)+len(increment)+opcode.OP_JUMP_LEN)...)
    }
    increment = append(increment, opcode.Make(opcode.OpJumpBack,
        len(test)+len(body)+len(increment))...)

    ins = append(init, test...)
    ins = append(ins, body...)
    ins = append(ins, increment...)

    return
}
```

fix jumps

Let's take a look at `fixJumps()` (also in compiler/flow.go).

```go
func (c *Compiler) fixJumps(
    ins opcode.Instructions,
    conditionalJumps bool,
    lookForOperandCode int, decrementCnt *int,
    jumpLocal, jumpNonLocal, frameLevel int) opcode.Instructions {

    opJumpLocal := opcode.OpJump
    opJumpNonLocal := opcode.OpJumpRelay
    if conditionalJumps {
        opJumpLocal = opcode.OpJumpIfNotTruthy
        opJumpNonLocal = opcode.OpJumpRelayIfNotTruthy
    }

    // currently lacking an intermediate rep. (IR) compilation phase, ...
    // ... we convert the bytecode into slices first
    insSlc := opcode.OpCodesAndOperandsSliceOfInstructionSlices(ins)
```

This starts by generating a new slice, each element of which contains one opcode and all of its operands. Then, we begin creating a new set of bytecode instructions.

```go
    newIns := opcode.Instructions{}

    for _, piece := range insSlc {
        if frameLevel == 0 {
            jumpLocal -= len(piece)
        }
        newPiece := piece // unless we find out otherwise
```

You'll notice that if we're at frame level 0, we decrement the `jumpLocal` distance for each instruction so that we set the relative jump accurately. When we call `fixJumps()` from itself (on a scoped set of instructions), we increment the frame level (passing `frameLevel+1`, as you'll see), which causes the latter-called `fixJumps()` to stop decrementing the `jumpLocal` distance.

In the `range insSlc` loop, we check for an OpJumpPlaceHolder and whether it has the operand we're looking for.

```
switch piece[0] {
case opcode.OpJumpPlaceHolder:
    operand := int(opcode.ReadUInt32(piece[1:]))

    if operand == lookForOperandCode {
        if frameLevel == 0 {
            newPiece = opcode.Make(opJumpLocal, jumpLocal)

        } else {
            if jumpNonLocal == 0 {
                newPiece = opcode.Make(
                    opJumpNonLocal, jumpLocal, frameLevel)

            } else {
                newPiece = opcode.Make(
                    opJumpNonLocal, jumpNonLocal, frameLevel)
            }
        }
        if decrementCnt != nil {
            (*decrementCnt)--
        }
    }
}
// else...
// maybe another placeholder type ... pass it through...
```

This checks the frame level before replacing a placeholder. If it is level 0, it can use a simple OpJump, but if another frame level, we can't just jump, as it would make no sense. We have to jump out of the current frame **and** jump past instructions. We use OpJumpRelay, which has 2 operands, one for the frame level and one for the jump distance. This opcode will cause the VM to back out the frame level specified, then jump. We'll see more about this in the "if / given expressions" chapter.

Note that one thing that makes it possible to replace these instructions this way (and for other jump instructions to still be accurate) is that jump opcodes, with their operands, all use the same amount of bytes. Looking at the operands and their widths, you can see that OpJumpRelay's first operand uses 1 byte less than OpJump's 1 operand. This leaves room for OpJumpRelay to use 1 more byte to indicate the frame level, and end up using the same amount of bytes as OpJump. OpJumpPlaceHolder uses more bytes than would be necessary for it's operand, just for the purpose of reserving space for OpJump or OpJumpRelay.

Having replaced a placeholder, we decrement the count (based on being passed a pointer to an integer) to end up with 0 when the compiler is done (if all is well). These would be the `breakStmtCount` and `nextStmtCount` mentioned a short while ago (and `fallthroughStmtCount`, which we haven't yet discussed in this book).

When checking deeper scope, we change instructions in constants that were compiled earlier. They're not "constant" yet.

```
case opcode.OpExecute:
    index := opcode.ReadUInt16(piece[1:])

    c.constants[index].(*object.CompiledCode).Instructions =
        c.fixJumps(
            c.constants[index].(*object.CompiledCode).Instructions,
            conditionalJumps, lookForOperandCode, decrementCnt,
            jumpLocal, jumpNonLocal, frameLevel+1)
```

When calling itself, we make sure to increase the frame level variable and we pass along the `jump` distance as we have determined it to this point.

We use the same technique on instructions referenced by OpTryCatch. We will see the *try/catch/else* sections in the "exceptions" chapter.

```
case opcode.OpTryCatch:
    tryIndex := opcode.ReadUInt16(piece[1:])
    catchIndex := opcode.ReadUInt16(piece[3:])
    elseIndex := opcode.ReadUInt16(piece[5:])

    c.constants[tryIndex].(*object.CompiledCode).Instructions =
        c.fixJumps(
            c.constants[tryIndex].(*object.CompiledCode).Instructions,
            conditionalJumps, lookForOperandCode, decrementCnt,
            jumpLocal, jumpNonLocal, frameLevel+1)

    c.constants[catchIndex].(*object.CompiledCode).Instructions =
        c.fixJumps(
            c.constants[catchIndex].(*object.CompiledCode).Instructions,
            conditionalJumps, lookForOperandCode, decrementCnt,
            jumpLocal, jumpNonLocal, frameLevel+1)

    if elseIndex != 0 {
        c.constants[elseIndex].(*object.CompiledCode).Instructions =
            c.fixJumps(
                c.constants[elseIndex].(*object.CompiledCode).Instructions,
                conditionalJumps, lookForOperandCode, decrementCnt,
                jumpLocal, jumpNonLocal, frameLevel+1)
    }
}
```

We append the instruction set on each iteration through the instruction slice, and finally return them at the end of `fixJumps()`.

```
        newIns = append(newIns, newPiece...)
    }

    return newIns
}
```

Finally, we've learned about compiling langur *for* loops with `break` and `next` statements.

14

if / given expressions

Besides *if* expressions, many languages also have a *switch* statement (as we've already seen that Go has), or something similar. Langur's *switch* is called "given." A *given* expression is highly flexible and expressive, but the reality is that it is almost entirely a glorified *if* expression. Fallthrough is the exception, as it is not allowed on an *if* expression. (This is important to langur, because langur allows fallthrough from anywhere within a *given* expression block, and it may be contained within an *if* expression that's within a *given* expression.) Since *given* expressions are mostly a semantic convenience, the parser converts a *given* expression node to an *if* expression node, so that the compiler never sees it. We compile an *if* expression and check for fallthrough only if it's from a *given* expression. So, we'll mostly ignore *given* expressions from here.

You'll note that I'm calling them "expressions." Treating *if* and *switch* as statements or expressions varies between languages. In langur, they always produce something, even if it's nothing. If there is no `else` (or `default` for *given*), we add an implicit *else* producing `null`.

The opcode layout of a langur *if* expression looks like the following, with at least one and possibly multiple test and action sections, but always one elseAction section. A failed test jumps to the next test. A final failed test jumps to the elseAction section. If we have a successful test, we execute the opcodes for the action, which is followed by an unconditional jump to get out. The elseAction section doesn't need a jump to get out, as it ends the expression.

1. test n
    conditional jump to next test (or to elseAction if final test)
2. action n
    unconditional jump out
   (rinse, repeat ...)
3. elseAction

This may look simpler than the *for* loops we looked at earlier, but compiling it is more difficult.

We have some complications in compiling scoped *if* expressions in langur, since it uses frames for scope, and each test/action of an *if* expression is scoped separately. We'll get to that, but we'll start with opcodes of *if* expressions containing no scope (no declarations).

simple, non-scoped if expression opcodes

```
>> val .x = 3
    ...
>> if .x > 7 { true } else if .x == 7 { false }
   # note: same as given .x { case > 7: true; case 7: false }

ByteCode Instructions
0000 GetGlobal 4
0003 Constant 2
0006 GreaterThan 0 0
0010 JumpIfNotTruthy 6
0015 True
0016 Jump 22
0021 GetGlobal 4
0024 Constant 2
0027 Equal 0 0
0031 JumpIfNotTruthy 6
0036 False
```

```
0037 Jump 1
0042 Null
0043 Pop

ByteCode Constants
1: Number 3
2: Number 7
```

You see jumps and other simple instructions, as the VM knows nothing about the fancy *if* expression. So, first we get `.x` (`0000 GetGlobal 4`), compare it to 7 (`0003 Constant 2` then `0006 GreaterThan 0 0`), and jump to the next test section if it doesn't compare (`0010 JumpIfNotTruthy 6`). Remember that conditional jumps pop the item they're testing off the stack, whether the test succeeds or fails. The full length, with operands, of the OpJumpIfNotTruthy code being 5 and starting at 0010, this conditionally jumps to `0021` (`0010 + 5 + 6`). If it's good, we don't jump yet. We keep reading instructions from where we are to get our result. Once we have a result, we must jump over the remaining opcodes that make up our *if* expression (`0016 Jump 22`, or `0037 Jump 1`). Get me out of here! ... so to speak. We repeat this pattern for the next test and result until we're done. Then we have our result at the top of the stack. We finally see a pop at the end, but it's not part of the *if* expression, but there because we're done. (We can use *if* or *given* expressions in the middle of other expressions and these would not pop, but rather use the result.) The `0042 Null` is our implicit elseAction section, since we didn't specify one using `else` and the *if* expression must return something.

scoped if expression opcodes

With scope, things get complicated. Here's a simple example of our opcodes and constants.

I use the following langur function for extracting the Unicode version from a file.

```
val .unicodeVersion = f(.row) {
    if val .matches = submatch(RE/(?i)-(\d+\.\d+\.\d+)\.txt/, .row) {
        return .matches[1]
    }
    throw "error getting Unicode version"
}
```

Let us go to the REPL and use part of the code above (shortening the variable name `.matches` to `.m` so it fits on one line in the printed book without wrapping).

```
>> val .row = "# Blocks-11.0.0.txt"
    ...
>> if val .m = submatch(RE/(?i)-(\d+\.\d+\.\d+)\.txt/, .row) { .m[1] }
ByteCode Instructions
0000 Execute 4
0003 Jump 1
0008 Null
0009 Pop

ByteCode Constants
1: String "# Blocks-11.0.0.txt"
2: Regex Re2 "(?i)-(\\d+\\.\\d+\\.\\d+)\\.txt"
3: Number 1
4: Code (...); LocalBindingsCount: 1
Instructions
0000 GetBuiltIn 83
0003 Constant 2
0006 GetGlobal 4
0009 Call 2
0011 SetLocal 0
```

```
0013 JumpRelayIfNotTruthy 5 1
0018 GetLocal 0
0020 Constant 3
0023 Index
```

You'll notice that most of the instructions are in constant 4, rather than the global instruction set. Our *test* includes a declaration, and this requires the test and action to be wrapped into scope together (`0000 Execute 4`). If a test had no declarations, but its action did, then only the action would be wrapped in scope.

We start constant 4's instructions with `0000 GetBuiltIn 83`. In this case, it retrieves the built-in `submatch()` function. This number may be different for you.

Next we have `0003 Constant 2`. This is a pre-compiled re2 regex object, which you can see in the list of constants. The compiler was able to pre-compile it so that the VM doesn't have to (might slow it down if repeatedly compiling the same regex pattern).

The `0006 GetGlobal 4` retrieves the global value of `.row`, which is "# Blocks-11.0.0.txt".

Now, on the stack we've added the `submatch()` function, then 2 arguments to it (the regex object and the global). The `0009 Call 2` tells the VM that the last 2 objects we added are arguments.... You know the drill by now....

Having the result, we set `.m` with `0011 SetLocal 0`. Assignment being an expression, the value remains on the stack. We ask if the value is truthy with `0013 JumpRelayIfNotTruthy 5 1`, and use a jump relay if it is not. Being a conditional jump, this pops the value it checks off of the stack.

A jump relay sounds like an athletic event, doesn't it? As we touched on earlier, this is a jump across frame levels first, then instructions. So, `JumpRelayIfNotTruthy 5 1` means, if "not truthy," to jump one frame level, then 5 bytes. If we go back to the global instructions (1 frame level), we see right after the OpExecute an OpJump, which jumps out of the *if* expression. Since a failed test should send us to the next test, or to an elseAction, we want to jump over this jump so that we don't jump out. This jump relay does this for us.

To get the indexed value (`.m[1]`), we start by putting the `.m` array onto the stack with `0018 GetLocal 0`. Then we push the index to use (`0020 Constant 3`). Then we use OpIndex.

Having run out of instructions in that block of code, we fall back to the previous instructions. Since we had success and no jump relay, we jump out of the *if* expression (`0003 Jump 1`), over the implicit elseAction `null` (`0008 Null`).

compiling if expressions

Those examples give us enough to start discussing how to compile these things. *If* expressions are probably the most complicated thing we compile in langur (so far), so if you can understand these without a problem, the rest will be a breeze.

Each section of an *if* expression gets it's own scope. We compile each to one of the following.

1. no scope wrapping (no declarations in test or action)
2. wrap scope over test and action (declarations in test and possibly in action)
3. wrap scope over action only (declarations in action, but none in the test)

We loop through the `node.TestsAndActions` (node type `*ast.IfNode`) slice 3 times. It contains a slice of a `TestDo` struct for each test and action (see the ast package). For an *else/ default* section, the `Test` node will be `nil`.

```
type TestDo struct {
    Test Node
    Do   Node
}

type IfNode struct {
    Token           token.Token
    TestsAndActions []TestDo
    IsGivenExpr     bool
}
```

Please open compiler/flow.go in your IDE and locate `compileIfExpression()`. First, you see that we add an implicit *else/default* section if none is present.

```go
func (c *Compiler) compileIfExpression(node *ast.IfNode) (
    ins opcode.Instructions, err error) {

    if node.TestsAndActions[len(node.TestsAndActions)-1].Test != nil {
        node.TestsAndActions = append(node.TestsAndActions,
            ast.TestDo{
                Test: nil,
                Do: &ast.BlockNode{Statements: []ast.Node{ast.NoValue}},
            })
    }
```

We compile *if* expressions in 3 general steps (with 3 loops in `compileIfExpression()`). These are roughly represented in the slices we build at the beginning.

```go
type compiled struct {
    ins opcode.Instructions
    st  *SymbolTable
}
compiledTests := make([]compiled, len(node.TestsAndActions))
compiledActions := make([]compiled, len(node.TestsAndActions))
compiledTA := make([]compiled, len(node.TestsAndActions))
```

We compile test nodes first. That's the easy part. Looking inside the first loop, with `i` and `ta` as loop variables, we have....

```go
lastOne := i == len(node.TestsAndActions)-1

compiledTests[i].st = nil

if ta.Test == nil {
    if !lastOne {
        // Houston, we have a bug.
            ...
    }
```

```
} else {
    if ast.NodeContainsFirstScopeLevelDeclaration(ta.Test, 0) {
        // push and pop and save symbol table; wrap test/action later
        c.pushVariableScope(false)
        compiledTests[i].ins, err = c.compileNode(ta.Test, false)
        compiledTests[i].st = c.symbolTable // save table for re-use
        c.popVariableScope()

    } else {
        // no scope on test
        compiledTests[i].ins, err = c.compileNode(ta.Test, false)
    }
    if err != nil {
        return
    }
}
```

When we check ast.NodeContainsFirstScopeLevelDeclaration(), we're asking if we need to use scope on a section of code. If not, we can leave it without this complication (possibly less work for the VM).

In this code, we see something we haven't. We're saving the symbol table for reuse. This is only necessary if the test section has a declaration. If the action has declarations, but not the test, then only the action will need scope. Either way, we're not ready to use the wrapInstructions() method, as we don't have all the instructions to wrap yet.

Besides efficiency, a reason not to use scope on a test without declarations is that we need to jump over a test if there is a fallthrough in a *given* expression. *Given* expressions don't allow declarations in any test for this very reason.

Now, in our second loop, we compile the action nodes.

```
compiledActions[i].st = nil

// push scope?
if compiledTests[i].st != nil {
    // declarations in the test section and possibly in the action
    // using saved symbol table
    c.pushVariableScopeWithTable(compiledTests[i].st)
    compiledActions[i].st = c.symbolTable

} else if ast.NodeContainsFirstScopeLevelDeclaration(ta.Do, 0) {
    // declarations in the action, but not the test section
    // using new symbol table
    c.pushVariableScope(false)
    compiledActions[i].st = c.symbolTable
}
```

We start by testing to see if we used a new symbol table in compiling a test. If so, we must reuse the table for compiling the action. That is because variables declared in the test must be available in the action. If not using the same symbol table, the compiler would be lost (not "The Minnow"). If we didn't use a symbol table for the test, we still might need to push scope, if the action contains declarations.

```
compiledActions[i].ins, err = c.compileBlock(ta.Do.(*ast.BlockNode), true)
if err != nil {
    return
}

if compiledActions[i].st != nil {
    if compiledTests[i].st == nil {
        // wrap only action into scope, not the test
        compiledActions[i].ins =
            c.wrapInstructionsWithExecute(compiledActions[i].ins)
    }
    c.popVariableScope()
}
```

After determining whether to push scope or not, we finally compile a particular action. When that's over, we must pop scope if, and only if, we pushed one. Also, we ask if we had an action with scope, but not a test. If so, we go ahead and wrap the action instructions. If the test had scope, we're still not ready to wrap the test and action together. (We will do so in the third loop.)

Having compiled the actions and still in the second loop, we add to our tests conditional jumps over actions.

```
if len(compiledTests[i].ins) > 0 {
    // not "else" or "default"
    if compiledTests[i].st == nil {
        compiledTests[i].ins = append(compiledTests[i].ins,
            opcode.Make(opcode.OpJumpIfNotTruthy,
                len(compiledActions[i].ins)+jumpToEndOpCodeLen(i))...)

    } else {
        compiledTests[i].ins = append(compiledTests[i].ins,
            opcode.Make(opcode.OpJumpPlaceHolder,
                opcode.OC_PlaceHolder_IfElse_TestFailed)...)
    }
}
```

In adding a conditional jump over an action, we check if a test is buried in scope (if `compiledTests[i].st != nil`), and if it is, we use an OpJumpPlaceHolder with a specific code for the operand. This is because we don't know where to jump to yet. We go ahead and add this, so that we can calculate other jumps, and it has to be added at some point.

Finally, in our third loop, we assemble the pieces and almost finish them.

First, we check if we have a *given* expression, and if so, fix fallthrough jumps (already compiled to an OpJumpPlaceHolder with a code to indicate fallthrough). We waited until this point so that test and action section lengths would be known (mostly). We need to fix these jumps now, before we assemble the pieces.

```
if node.IsGivenExpr {
    if compiledTests[i].st != nil {
        err = makeErr(node,
            "Cannot use declarations in case statement of given")
        return
    }

    // not looking for fallthrough in default section
    if !lastOne {
        compiledActions[i].ins = c.fixJumps(
            compiledActions[i].ins, false,
            opcode.OC_PlaceHolder_Fallthrough, &c.fallthroughStmtCount,

            len(compiledActions[i].ins)+        // over current action
                jumpToEndOpCodeLen(i)+          // over jump to end
                len(compiledTests[i+1].ins),    // over next test

            0, 0)
    }
}
```

We disallow declarations in *case* statements of *given* expressions, because it would be difficult to set jumps if the next test is contained in a scope block (contained declarations). (Fallthrough jumps over tests.) Who needs declarations in *case* statements, anyway?

See the description of `fixJumps()` in the section about compiling *for* loops. In calculating the distance for a fallthrough jump, we used the function `jumpToEndOpCodeLen()` (shown on the next page). This returns 0 or the total length of a jump opcode, depending on whether the action already ends with a *break, next, fallthrough. throw,* or *return* statement. If it ends with one of these, adding a jump opcode to the end would be pointless, as it would never be reached.

```
jumpToEndOpCodeLen := func(i int) int {
    if ast.EndsWithDefiniteJump(
        node.TestsAndActions[i].Do.(*ast.BlockNode).Statements) {
        return 0
    } else {
        return opcode.OP_JUMP_LEN
    }
}
```

We're almost there. Still in the third loop, having fixed *fallthrough* jumps for *given* expressions, we put together the test and action instructions.

```
compiledTA[i].ins = append(compiledTests[i].ins, compiledActions[i].ins...)
```

Once we have the them combined, we can finally check to see if we need to wrap them together into a scope block. We know by checking whether we saved a symbol table for the test.

```
if compiledTests[i].st != nil {
    // wrap test and action into scope together
    c.pushVariableScopeWithTable(compiledTests[i].st)
    compiledTA[i].ins = c.wrapInstructionsWithExecute(compiledTA[i].ins)
    c.popVariableScope()

    compiledTA[i].ins = c.fixJumps(
        compiledTA[i].ins, true,
        opcode.OC_PlaceHolder_IfElse_TestFailed, nil,
        len(compiledTA[i].ins), jumpToEndOpCodeLen(i), 0)
}
```

In this case, we use the push and pop scope functions so the `wrapInstructionsWithExecute()` method will have the right variable counts to set for the scope block.

Then, we use `fixJumps()` to replace our test failed jump placeholders (which are now wrapped into a scope block). If you look back, you'll see we only used placeholders for these if we knew the test had scope. If it did not, we were able to set the jumps at that time.

Finally, we add placeholders for unconditional jumps that we talked about earlier, to jump out of an *if* expression, by adding them to the combined test/action sections.

```
if !lastOne {
    if jumpToEndOpCodeLen(i) > 0 {
        compiledTA[i].ins = append(compiledTA[i].ins,
            opcode.Make(opcode.OpJumpPlaceHolder,
                opcode.OC_PlaceHolder_IfElse_Exit)...)
    }
}
```

We use placeholders because we don't know the total expression length yet. Then, we build a single instruction set to return.

```
ins = append(ins, compiledTA[i].ins...)
```

And finally, after loop 3, now knowing the instruction length of the entire *if* expression, we fix jumps we set placeholders with in loop 3 (the jump to the end placeholders) and return the instructions.

```
    ins = c.fixJumps(
        ins, false, opcode.OC_PlaceHolder_IfElse_Exit,
        nil, len(ins), 0, 0)

    return
}
```

That was not easy, but it gives us *if* expressions with each test/action having its own scope.

15

exceptions

Langur uses exceptions instead of error return values. I've read about having to "unwind" a stack, traversing it twice, etc. to make exceptions work. None of that is necessary for langur. I suppose it helps that we're piggybacking Go's built-in memory management. It also helps that we use a separate frame for a *try* section and that backing out of a frame, it's values are automatically "popped."

Langur generally converts Go panics into langur exceptions. This might change. It does not catch out-of-memory panics, because there is no way to do so in Go 1 (according to what I've read).

Semantically, langur code does not use explicit *try* blocks. All the statements preceding a *catch* block within a block of code are an implicit *try* block. Being a scripting language, this can make for nicer coding. You could use a *catch* at the end of a script that covers the entire script, as just one example. To simulate an explicit *try* block, you could wrap it into a scope block (surround with curly braces).

Langur also allows a scoped *else* section at the end of a *catch*, as code to execute only if there was no exception. It is optional.

A *try/catch* in langur, with an *else* section, looks something like the following.

```
123 / 0

catch .e {
    if .e["cat"] == "math" {
        writeln "math exception!"
    } else {
        throw
    }
} else {
    # no exception
    writeln "just cruising along"
}
```

Note that the *try* section is implied.

try/catch in the VM

In the instruction loop, we read operands for OpTryCatch, giving us indices into the constants slice that point at CompiledCode objects containing separate opcode instructions for each part.

```
case opcode.OpTryCatch:
    tryIndex   := int(opcode.ReadUInt16(ins[ip+1:]))
    catchIndex := int(opcode.ReadUInt16(ins[ip+3:]))
    elseIndex  := int(opcode.ReadUInt16(ins[ip+5:]))
    ip += 6

    fnReturn, relay, err = vm.executeTryCatch(
        fr, tryIndex, catchIndex, elseIndex)
```

From vm.executeTryCatch(), langur uses a non-scoped frame to capture the result of the *try* block. When this frame returns, it checks if it received an error from it and if so, executes the *catch* frame. If there was no error and there is an *else* object (which is optional), it executes the code of the *else* object. The *else* has scope, so we go ahead and use a frame. (It's also convenient for this.) A *catch* is always scoped for the exception variable, so a frame is always appropriate for it as well. It calls vm.runCompiledCode() with *try*, and possibly *catch* or *else* code objects. As was shown in the chapter on "the VM," the vm.`runCompiledCode`() function will take care of generating and using frames.

```
func (vm *VM) executeTryCatch(
    fr *frame, tryIndex, catchIndex, elseIndex int) (
    fnReturn object.Object, relay *jumpRelay, err error) {

    tryCode := vm.constants[tryIndex].(*object.CompiledCode)

    fnReturn, relay, err = vm.runCompiledCode(tryCode, fr, nil, nil)
    if err == nil {
        if elseIndex != 0 {
            // else block used to run only when there is no exception
            elseCode := vm.constants[elseIndex].(*object.CompiledCode)
            fnReturn, relay, err = vm.runCompiledCode(
                elseCode, fr, nil, nil)
        }

    } else {
        catchCode := vm.constants[catchIndex].(*object.CompiledCode)

        // catch error returned from try frame
        // The error variable is a langur hash that is guaranteed ...
        // ... to contain certain keys, even if they have no data.
        errObj := object.NewErrorFromAnything(err, "")
        // compiler set up late-binding assignment in catch code, ...
        // ... so pass exception hash to be pushed onto the stack ...
        // ... of the catch frame (errObj.Contents)

        fnReturn, relay, err =
            vm.runCompiledCode(
                catchCode, fr, nil, []object.Object{errObj.Contents})
    }

    return
}
```

The object package new error functions convert an object and ensure that its error hash contains certain fields (such as "cat" and "msg") of certain types that langur guarantees. One could throw a hash that also contains other fields if he wants. We will see why we pass the error hash to vm.runCompiledCode() shortly.

throw in the VM

Again in the instruction loop, we have a case for OpThrow.

```
case opcode.OpThrow:
    err = vm.throw(fr, vm.pop())
```

And a method called throw()....

```
func (vm *VM) throw(fr *frame, what object.Object) error {
    errObj := object.NewErrorFromObject(what)

    // write function name to hash if source not already set (not ZLS)
    src, err := errObj.Contents.GetValue(object.ERR_HASHKEY_SOURCE)
    if err != nil {
        err = fmt.Errorf(
            "Error retrieving Error Object Source: %s", err.Error())
        bug("vm.throw", err.Error())
        return err
    }
    if src.(*object.String).Value == "" {
        errFnName, ok := fr.getFnName()
        if ok {
            errObj.Contents.WritePair(
                object.ERR_HASHKEY_SOURCE,
                object.NewString("."+errFnName))
        }
    }
    return errObj
}
```

This uses `object.NewErrorFromObject()`, to ensure that the object thrown matches the guarantees langur makes about it. It also sets the function name in the source of the thrown object unless the source field is already set (not a zero-length string). Then, it simply returns the error object. Seeing that we set the `err` variable in the instruction loop to the return value of `vm.throw()`, it will treat it as a langur exception from there.[14]

try/catch/throw opcodes

Let us try a *catch* in the REPL. Pun intended. We'll simplify the code example by using the implicit exception variable `.err` and a single expression (no curly braces around *catch* block), but the opcodes will look the same as if we had written it in the longer form.

```
>> 4/0; catch if .err["cat"]=="math" {writeln .err["msg"]} else {throw}
ByteCode Instructions
0000 TryCatch 3 7 0
0005 Pop

ByteCode Constants
1: Number 4
2: Number 0
3: Code (...)
0000 Constant 1
0003 Constant 2
0006 Divide

4: String "cat"
5: String "math"
6: String "msg"
7: Code (...); LocalBindingsCount: 1
0000 SetLocal 0
0002 Pop
0003 GetLocal 0
0005 Constant 4
```

---

14 You could think of *throw* as an explicit exception.

```
0008 Index
0009 Constant 5
0012 Equal 0 0
0016 JumpIfNotTruthy 16
0021 GetBuiltIn 102
0024 GetLocal 0
0026 Constant 6
0029 Index
0030 Call 1
0032 Jump 3
0037 GetLocal 0
0039 Throw

DivisionByZero
langur escaped result: DivisionByZero\n
```

First, we see `0000 TryCatch 3 7 0`. So, we know the *try* code is in constant 3 and the *catch* code in constant 7. The `0` operand indicates that there is no *else* code. This is okay, because an *else* code block will never be constant 0. (Something else would always be put into the constants slice first. We check for this in the compiler, just to ensure it doesn't become a bug.)

Looking at constant 3...

```
3: Code (...)
0000 Constant 1
0003 Constant 2
0006 Divide
```

You can see that this is not a scoped block (no local bindings count as there is on constant 7). The rest is rather self-explanatory at this point. We push two constants onto the stack, then use OpDivide to calculate the result. OpDivide will pop two values off the top of the objects stack, calculate the result, and push it onto the stack.

So, what happens when OpDivide fails? The VM receives the error from its call to do the division. When the VM receives an error, it exits the current frame, returning the error message. In this case, it is our *try* frame. Looking back at the `executeTryCatch()` method, we see it checks for an error when the *try* frame exits. If it receives one, then it executes the *catch* frame. An error could have propagated out of several frames until it was caught by executeTryCatch( ). I'm thinking this is much simpler than exceptions in some other languages.

Let's look at the *catch* frame. We see that it starts with...

```
0000 SetLocal 0
0002 Pop
```

These are the opcodes to set the exception variable. This is different than we've seen, as there are no opcode instructions to push anything onto the stack before we set a variable and pop off the object. How do we know what we're setting the variable to? In this case, we've sent a slice of objects (with one object) with our error hash to the vm.runCompiledCode( ) method.

```
fnReturn, relay, err =
    vm.runCompiledCode(catchCode, fr, nil, []object.Object{errObj.Contents})
```

The vm.runCompiledCode( ) method will pass the "late" slice to the vm.newFrame( ) method, which will push these objects onto the stack before vm.runCompiledCode( ) starts executing instructions. So, we know the error hash is at the top of the stack before the OpSetLocal is executed, and then OpPop pops it off.

At the end of the *if* expression ending the *catch* frame, we see it re-throwing the exception variable. (A throw token without specifying anything implicitly re-throws the exception, so it may propagate until it is caught by another *try/catch*, or is not caught and the script exits with an error.) The OpGetLocal is there to grab the exception variable to re-throw. (It may be implicit in langur source code, but it must be explicit to the VM.)

```
0037 GetLocal 0
0039 Throw
```

An OpThrow generates a langur error object from whatever is at the top of the stack, and returns it as a Go error from the current frame. It is able to return this object as a Go error because langur error objects satisfy both interfaces (Error and langur's object.Object).[15]

compiling throw

As I write, `compileTryCatch()` and `compileThrow()` are in the compiler/flow.go file.

We'll look first at `compileThrow()`, because it's so simple.

```go
func (c *Compiler) compileThrow(node *ast.ThrowNode) (
    ins opcode.Instructions, err error) {

    ins, err = c.compileNode(node.Exception, false)
    if err != nil {
        return
    }
    ins = append(ins, opcode.Make(opcode.OpThrow)...)
    return
}
```

The parser has neatly packaged the thing to throw (`node.Exception`) with the `*ast.ThrowNode`, even if implicitly re-throwing the exception received. So, we simply compile that first, specifying not to add an OpPop if it might, then append one more instruction (OpThrow). We know our value will then be at the top of the stack, ready to be thrown, when the OpThrow instruction is reached by the VM.

compiling try/catch

Now, let's look at `compileTryCatch()`. While we don't have an explicit *try* section semantically in langur code, the parser neatly packages our *try*, *catch*, and *else* in an

---

15 To satisfy the Error interface, all you have to do is include a method called Error() that returns a Go string.

`*ast.TryCatchNode` so the compiler has something to work with. (Parsers, always looking out for us.)

```go
func (c *Compiler) compileTryCatch(node *ast.TryCatchNode) (
    ins opcode.Instructions, err error) {

    var try, catch, tcelse opcode.Instructions

    try, err = c.compileNode(node.Try, false)
    if err != nil {
        return
    }
    tryIndex := c.addConstant(&object.CompiledCode{Instructions: try})
```

We start by compiling the *try* node, adding it to the constants slice (using a CompiledCode object), and saving the index for later. Pretty simple. Note that we pass false when compiling the *try* (as we also do with *catch* and *else* sections), as we want its value to remain on the stack.

Then, we push scope for the *catch* frame, as it will always have scope, at the least for the exception hash variable. We compile exception variable instructions as a declaration assignment statement and save them to a variable called `setException`.

```go
// push scope for the catch frame, including the exception variable
c.pushVariableScope(false)
defer c.popVariableScope()

var setException opcode.Instructions
if node.ExceptionVar != nil {
    setException, err = c.compileNode(
        ast.MakeDeclarationAssignmentStatement(
            node.ExceptionVar, nil, true, false),
        true)

    if err != nil {
        return
    }
}
```

Before we compile the exception assignment with `compileNode()`, we build more tree nodes by calling `ast.MakeDeclarationAssignmentStatement()`. We pass `true` for "system assignment" and `false` for "mutable." Passing `node.ExceptionVar` for the variable, but `nil` for a tree node to set it to, we get an assignment without any preceding instructions. Thus, the OpSetLocal 0 at the very beginning of *catch* frame opcodes. It's in the `nil`. At risk of repeating myself, we can do this because we will push the value onto the stack before starting execution of the instructions. We pass `true` to `compileNode()` for setting the exception variable so it can add OpPop at the end of the declaration assignment statement.

Having compiled exception variable setting instructions and saving them, we can move on to compiling the rest of the *catch*. You'll remember we pushed scope before setting up the exception variable, and haven't popped it yet.

```
catch, err = c.compileNode(node.Catch, false)
if err != nil {
    return
}
if node.ExceptionVar != nil {
    catch = append(setException, catch...)
}
catchIndex := c.wrapInstructions(catch)
```

To wrap the *catch* in scope, we don't use `wrapInstructionsWithExecute()`, as that would return an OpExecute instruction, which we don't want or need in this case. We want an index. We use `wrapInstructions()`, which will "wrap" the instructions by placing them into a CompiledCode object, setting the locals count properly according to the current symbol table, adding this object to the constants slice, and returning the index to the constant.

Next, we compile the *else* instructions, if there are any. We pushed scope for the *catch*, so we must pop and push scope again, as the *else* section has its own scope and is outside of the *catch* scope. The `defer` we set earlier will still run as we exit, and pop this last scope.

```
    elseIndex := 0
    if node.Else != nil {
        // pop scope from catch; else with different scope
        c.popVariableScope()
        c.pushVariableScope(false)

        tcelse, err = c.compileNode(node.Else, false)
        elseIndex = c.wrapInstructions(tcelse)
        if elseIndex == 0 {
            bug("compileTryCatch",
                "elseIndex 0 (0 used as indicator for no else section)")
        }
    }

    ins = opcode.Make(opcode.OpTryCatch, tryIndex, catchIndex, elseIndex)
    return
}
```

Having compiled *try*, *catch*, and *else* sections and saving indices for them, we have only one instruction to return from compileTryCatch(), an OpTryCatch with operands for the indices. And that's it.

fini

I wrote langur to develop skills for a programming project that I may get to someday.

Langur is open source, free software. Visit langurlang.org to see about the language or opcodebook.com for information about the book. Writing a book and trying to explain things helps you see things you missed. There were many changes and fixes to langur due to writing this book. Having been laid off and having no income, I realized I could write about langur and hope to make a useful book.

I hope you have found this useful. You won't find me on social media. Please feel free to contact me using the form at opcodebook.com with corrections, typos, etc.

That is all. When you're done, you should finish.

– Anthony

www.ingramcontent.com/pod-product-compliance
Lightning Source LLC
Chambersburg PA
CBHW060130060326
40690CB00018B/3823

9 781734 314502